IMPACT

A
Woman's
Guide
to
Impactful
Interactions!

Petra Weiser

IMPACT: A Woman's Guide to Impactful Interactions!

by Petra Weiser

Published by Petra Weiser LLC

Paperback ISBN: 978-1-7344038-5-5
Hardcover ISBN: 978-1-7344038-6-2
Kindle ISBN: 978-1-7344038-7-9
EPUB ISBN: 978-1-7344038-8-6

Cover Design by Annette Wood Graphics
www.annettewoodgraphics.com

Edited by Joanna Kneller
www.blueheronediting.com

DISCLAIMER

Following the advice in this book has the potential to transform your life. On the other hand, it may not, and you could hurt yourself in the process. So, regardless of the claim I just made—and the claims I made on the cover, back cover, and throughout this book—I make no claims. Use at your own risk. Your life is yours, and your decisions and actions are yours as well.

If things should work out well for you, please write a long five-star review on Amazon and spread the word about how my book alone completely transformed your life (like I said it would, by the way).

DEDICATION

For those willing to L.O.V.E.!
You are AWESOME!

DEDICATION

For those willing to O.V.E.
You are AWESOME!

TABLE OF CONTENTS

PREFACE

"Life is what you make of it,

not the other way around."

Petra Weiser

created this motto years ago when I finally figured out that I had control over a lot of things. "Things" in this instance doesn't mean the remote control, when to serve dinner, how to eat an Oreo cookie, or what clothes to wear the next day. I'm talking about the things that impact the direction of our lives with purpose. I'm here to tell you that you can do the same. Every chapter in this book is already part of your life. The only investments you must commit to are yourself, honesty, and time. The key to it all lies within you, and I am going to help you unlock your hidden powers. Change takes effort and courage to do something differently than before. You are ready, and I applaud you for picking up this book and for giving it (and yourself) a chance. You are worth it.

Interactions are part of our daily lives: At work, we communicate with colleagues, bosses, vendors, and customers. When not at work, we deal with spouses, partners, friends, family, as well as a broad multitude of strangers. As members of a society, we cannot avoid people. We must socialize. Unfortunately, after interactions with the not-so-pleasant individuals, we often walk away feeling overwhelmed, tired, discouraged, powerless, even unworthy. Other times, we simply fail to communicate clearly and with purpose, and encounters can result in misunderstandings, heated arguments, or physical altercations. I used to worry about meetings that could lead to conflict or ridicule, and I was an expert at finding ways to avoid the people who impacted me negatively. No more!

L.O.V.E. (Learn, Observe, Value, Empower), the process behind impactful interactions, will transform the way you act and react, and, most importantly, it will alter your approach to those interactions that matter most to you. Along this journey, we will strive to put your interest at the forefront, which is important if you want to take ownership of your life. Selfishness in this sense is a must. You lost sight of that somewhere in your past because our society expected you to conform. Unfortunately, that came with a price tag of your own worth and self-respect.

As you start reading, you may question the relevancy of the content and how it will affect your interactions. Trust the process. LEARN, the first chapter, outlines your willingness to learn as the foundation for any success. OBSERVE makes you look at everything differently, including yourself. VALUE puts a different spin on worth and worthiness. And finally, EMPOWER ties the concept together while serving as a call to action. Think of each chapter as a piece of the puzzle that will reveal the bigger picture in time.

I don't expect you to agree with everything. I am full of my own views and opinions—just like the rest of your world—and they may not be the same as yours. Take what works for you and discard the rest. But be honest enough to work through the places where you feel stuck or uncomfortable. There's a reason I may have hit a nerve.

My writing comes from a place of systemic oppression of women in our society by the patriarchy. I want you to become more aware of the many subtle ways this oppression has been woven into your own life. Your behavior has been influenced by a lot of external factors. Guilt and submission are tools used with purpose to keep women repressed. Take this opportunity to understand yourself better in your society to empower and support all women.

I should point out that I am not a psychologist, psychiatrist, or recognized expert in any field. However, I am EVERY woman. My process and findings have been derived from years of firsthand experiences. The L.O.V.E. process has worked for me. I owe my successes to these four steps. I am an average woman who isn't. Just like you.

Women are worth it. You are worth it.

Let's begin.

CHAPTER 1: LEARN

Life is about learning.

Granted, some people only learn the minimum to get by. Then they stop. This book is not for them.

I truly believe that we stop living when and if we stop learning.

Learning is the first step in cultivating your empowered self. This may sound boring, but it is what it is. And while it isn't the greatest revelation in the world, you know for a fact that you've come as far as you have because you were willing to learn (and adapt). That alone is awesome.

Learning is a huge topic, and this chapter will prove that point. That's because learning is the driving force behind empowerment. This book will help make your learning process more conscientious so that you can become aware quicker and with purpose. Awareness paves the path toward empowerment.

Before getting into the how, I want to establish what I consider to be the foundation for success. This foundation helps us make it through each day. There are three pillars, and you should have, at minimum, one of these to be a functional citizen in our society. These three pillars are our basic life skills.

Here they are in order:
1. Learning how to fit in.
2. Learning how to take care of yourself.
3. Learning how to take care of others.

I have intentionally used "learning" with each. That's because all of us have learned these skills (to some extent). You may have mastered the first one, yet with a feeling that it is not to your benefit.

Skills two and three are built on the first one. I am certain that you haven't mastered them. Despite that, we all have done well enough to ensure that our society functions. After all, societies are made of people, and people need to be able to take care of themselves (and others) as not to be a huge burden on society. The better functioning its citizens, the more prosperous the society. Of course, that doesn't mean there aren't a gazillion imbalances in our society, but I will let someone else write another book about that. You get the idea, I hope.

This foundation is the starting point we need to continue learning for our best benefits.

Let's take a closer look at the first pillar.

Fitting In (Family, Society, Culture, the World)

The learning process starts the minute you are born. That applies to you and your parents. On the one side, you are teaching them how to interact with you: You cry to get things you need. You want food, a clean diaper, to be held, to be put down, etc. That doesn't mean you should cry all the time when you want something, but let's keep that on the back burner for later. As a newborn, however, this is your preferred way of communication, and it is acceptable behavior (at first). It also plays into my earlier point of being selfish to take care of your own needs first. Obviously, you were born selfish for the simple reason to survive.

On the other side, your parents will let you know their expectations: when to be quiet, when to eat, when to sleep, when to wake up. Their expectations often do not align with yours, but this will help you to understand the meaning of good and bad timing as far as your own desires are concerned. It's all about the *when* in the very beginning to keep your parents sane. Additionally, you must be taught the *when* so that you know later *when* to do *what*.

Your childhood is filled with rules and your mostly unchallenged acceptance of them. Your parents (or the person trying to take care of you) will teach you the morals and societal expectations needed to make you a functional, law-abiding adult. As an adolescent, you may come to dislike the parental hovering and intrusion. They'll likely never stop telling you when to do what and how. Even when you're fifty.

With you fitting in, you'll also have to figure out your place in society. You won't so much care about this part until you get much older. *Screw society* will be your mantra for a good while in your teenage years. And honestly, it will last all your adult life (especially when doing your tax returns). Every society has rules, and everyone must abide by them or go to jail. So, you simmer down, and your expectation of acceptable behavior aligns with the society you happen to live in.

So . . . what is a society? A society is a region with people that share the same beliefs and values that are governed by rules/laws/guidelines. It is meant to unite the people living in it. Within each society, there is culture. Culture is where behavior is taught and then judged by society and where we also recognize differences in behaviors/looks/customs. Societies are super judgmental when it comes to culture, especially when there are a lot of different cultures living in one society. Confused yet? Culture represents a more specific set of values, behaviors, beliefs, objects, customs, etc. by a certain group of people, which then gets passed down generationally. Culture is the glue that holds societies together. Culture tells us how to behave while societies govern the framework for that behavior.

Naturally, if you don't agree with your culture or your society, then you can figure out if there's another place in the world that could be more appealing to your own cultural standards.

There are higher demands on women for fitting in, and in the quest to keep women in their assigned lanes—and within patriarchal expectations—society has ensured that a woman's life shall always be harder than a man's. It was designed that way, and if you don't know that, then you have a lot to learn. Keep reading.

There's such a double standard: Girls are taught what to wear or not to wear, what to say or not to say; they are expected to look pretty and behave perfectly all the time. They are discouraged from acting out or speaking up, and get chastised when they interrupt, and are told, "You can't do that." Think opposite for boys. Any behavior that is frowned upon for girls is mostly excused as "boys will be boys" for boys. Boys are leaders if they are strong-willed and tough; girls are bossy and emotional for the same behavior. This soundtrack is repeated over and over from birth. The system confirms all these societal and cultural expectations.

Our society supports the patriarchy. Our educational systems, our financial institutions, and our laws and rights were formed with purpose and intent to protect it. This protection has come at a high cost to women, who have been oppressed for ages in order to cling to the patriarchy.

Female oppression is systemic.

Below are just a few examples of women's past struggles:

It wasn't until the mid-1800s that more women were allowed access to higher education. In general, it was thought that women didn't have the brain capacity to learn. Then, middle- and upper-class white women in the so-called Republican Motherhood obtained a higher education to ensure that the next female generation would learn their place in the patriarchal society away from public life while, at the same time, helping their sons become future citizens of public life. The objective behind allowing women access to education was never to include them in public life where laws and rights were created and decided. Educated women then went on to establish female dame and boarding schools. First with the focus on furthering a woman's domestic skill set and behavior. Men feared that if women were taught more complex subjects (such as Latin, Greek, calculus, biology), it would lead to them having other radical ideas and thoughts. It took decades, and a feminist seminary movement, to truly advance real education for women so they could earn officially recognized college degrees.

The official women's suffrage movement started in 1848. Along the way, women also took up the fight against Black oppression and for enfranchising the Black vote, hoping to gain support for the female vote. If white men could grant voting rights to what they considered to be the lesser race, then the thought was that white women could be given the same rights. Yet women were still excluded from the voting club after the ratification of the 14th and 15th Amendments, which confirmed citizens to mean men only. It took another fifty-two years, after adding the 14th Amendment in 1868 that enabled Black men to vote, before women could head to the polls. Make no mistake about it:

Women weren't *given* the vote; women fought for it. In America, women couldn't vote until 1920 (in Switzerland, it was 1971!). Still, it took some states until the 1980s to fully ratify the 19th Amendment. What a shame! Only white MEN were created equal in the eyes of our original constitution, which held on to that viewpoint for centuries.

Women couldn't open bank accounts (or have credit cards) in the United States without their husbands' consent until the 1970s. It was thought that women could not be financially responsible.

To this date, no American woman can decide what to do with her own body. Think about it. Women can't get a hysterectomy without an acceptable reason, whereas a man can get a vasectomy without having to face any legal or social hurdles or consequences. Women are punished for having female parts without having any rights over them, and women's rights to this day are dependent on decisions and laws made mostly by men. The recently empowered anti-abortion movement and limitations imposed on women in general for seeking healthcare in the United States are proof.

Another tool for oppressing women came in the form of devaluing women's work and contributions during the industrial revolution. Housework paid no wage. No wage translated into zero value for the work performed. Yet nothing could be bought without money. Everything had to be purchased because nobody had a homestead anymore with a large garden or animals to self-sustain. Since the man earned money for his valuable work while his wife managed everything else at home for free, women became dependent on a man to provide.

When women did go to work, they were paid much less since they had little to no education and less skills. (Inequities in pay prevail to this day despite women's equal educational status and qualifications.) Some jobs that they were allowed to work were considered less important, like teaching, nursing, cleaning, and cooking. Women and certain jobs to date are continually undervalued on purpose. Women must work twice as hard for less money, and most of the time, women have to prove themselves to potential employers/bosses (whereas a man is taken by his word that he can perform the job based on hearsay).

Finally, and for many of you working *real* jobs, this will ring true and may be the reason you are reading this book: Women in the corporate world are continually overlooked, purposely ignored, and made out to be unstable and emotional wrecks. While a male supervisor can scream with spittle flying from his mouth and his arms gesticulating in all directions, nobody will ever consider him to be unstable.

Women hold these truths to be self-evident.

We ignore and excuse bad behavior by males because that's just the way it is. It isn't. Just because the majority of our society was brainwashed to believe that does not make it just or so.

Most men, and many women, do not spend any time thinking about the differences in gender behaviors and expectations. There are so many ways of saying something that is not true, but we believe it is since it has been repeated to us all our lives. This is where learning will be crucial. With knowledge comes power. The more you know, the more upset you will become because you have been excluded for too long.

Welcome to my club.

We need to acknowledge that women have much more to consider and worry about when trying to fit in. The expectations are so high. Women are taught from the get-go to not upset the applecart. We are truly good sheep. And we keep shooting ourselves in the foot because of it. My hope is that the more you learn, the more you will see and become aware of the way things are. And that we can impact change for the better.

Unlike the next two life skills, I will not dive deeper into how we fit in. Chances are, if you are reading this, you are an adult, and you have had plenty of exposure on the road to becoming a law-abiding, neighborly citizen. Fitting in—and how we fit in—is made possible thanks to parents, teachers, cultures, laws, values, and societies imparting on us the rules of fitting in through accepted behaviors, greater-good expectations, and lawful obedience. Granted, you may not fit in well—you may be the outcast, the oddball, the weirdo—nonetheless, you are functional in your society/community based on the framework of laws and regulations and expected behaviors.

Let's move on to the next two life skills as they can help you to impact change while fitting in so that your environment can adapt to you while also adjusting the parameters of the framework to be more inclusive.

Taking Care of Yourself

The goal is to be independent. Or, at least, it used to be. It was my biggest goal, seeing that my parents were super strict and controlling. These days, though, some parents are having a hard time getting their forty-year-old child to move out, along with the online gaming peripherals that must have cost a small mortgage (hence, preventing said child from moving out). Of course, it's hard to move out without a job. Or a driver's license.

I'm a bit confused over this development. I couldn't wait to get out of my parents' house to do as I pleased, and to prove to them—and the world—that I was quite capable of making something of myself without supervision and control.

I loathed the idea of scrounging off my parents (or anyone else) to make it through life. To some degree, I blame those parents. Have they learned nothing? They haven't (or at least the bare minimum), and so, the apple does not fall far from the tree. Do I need to point out that most of those apples are male?

Taking care of yourself must be a priority. At any stage in your life. This also includes a certain level of selfishness, and I will address this in this chapter.

There are two parts of taking care of yourself. The first encompasses the basics, which means you can make it through life every day—even if that life is a struggle. That's the fitting-in part. But there's so much more to life. The second aspect, the most important one for your self-development, is to practice self-care. It's exactly what it says: you taking care of you. With emphasis on CARE and YOU. I know so many friends and family members who always put others first. They have so much love and empathy (and sympathy), that they have made others their priority. They don't want to appear (or be) selfish. Selfishness is viewed as an egotistical trait. Yet selfishness is a dichotomy. There's a good and a bad side of it. When trying to live your life, who do you need to depend on the most? News flash (or not): The only person that can get you through your life is YOU. If you don't take care of yourself, you'll be lost, tired, depressed, weak, stuck, unmotivated. You get the idea.

I totally get that taking care of others ranks right up there along with self-care, but it does not take spot number one. Let's flip this thought around. Do you always want to be taken care of by others? Are you looking for someone else to step in all the time to offer you something that you may not need/want?

For example, during my last visit to Germany, I asked my sister for a protein snack recipe she had mentioned to me. She said right away, "I'll make some for tomorrow." I was stunned. It's not what I had asked for. I'm very direct, and if I wanted the snacks baked by tomorrow, I would have undoubtedly asked my sister to do so. But I didn't. I wanted to see the recipe so that I could decide whether they would be worthwhile baking because if the treats contained too much of the bad stuff (sugar, butter), then I wasn't interested. I said to her, "I don't want you to do that. I just want to see the recipe. Just send it to me. But don't go through the trouble of making them. REALLY!" In turn, she immediately responded, "Oh, it's no trouble at all." To which I said, "Even if it isn't, I don't want any. Okay?" My sister, of all people, should know that I mean what I say. There was no ambiguous intent in my words, silently begging her to go out of her way to please me. The next day she brought the recipe and a freshly baked batch, and unfortunately, the recipe confirmed that the snacks contained a lot of sugar and butter. The disappointment in my sister's eyes when I refused the treats hurt me as much as it did her. We both felt horrible, and one could argue that I should have just eaten a few pieces. But consider that you do not (and should not) go out of your way to please someone if (a) you told that someone that you didn't want what was offered, and (b) that action goes against your values (for me in this case, mindful eating was part of my self-care regimen). Additionally, at times, it is important to make a point. I needed my sister to know that she should respect other people's wishes. If I would have thanked her excessively, I would have reinforced her unwanted behavior, which means that she would continue to walk all over her internal battery for what she assumes to be a good deed.

Consider that, when giving or offering, you may be forcing yourself on others who really do not appreciate such overabundance of care or attention. Some people don't want to be rude and refuse, but wouldn't that be better than ending up with something they didn't want and that just depleted your battery? Respect what others ask of you—or what they do not ask of you—while evaluating the impact of your offering in regard to self-care.

Self-care really encompasses a lot, and I will expand on this next. In a nutshell, self-care is about everything that you can do for yourself to ensure that you are, and remain, healthy inside and out. Taking care of yourself means that you are not just functioning in your society but that you are thriving—and then you can take care of others as well. Got it?

How Do We Self-Care?

A note of encouragement before we venture on: First, do not become overwhelmed with this extensive list. The purpose is to show how many aspects of self-care there are, potentially in areas that you have never considered previously. Second, I'm not saying to do all of them, especially not all at once. Read through them and pick one that speaks to you. You should know which one you need the most, but consider that it may not be the best one to start with if it is not feasible to achieve under your current circumstance. You want to succeed, so start small. Every bit helps, and you will be creating a good foundation you can add to later.

Furthermore, some of the below suggestions will be easier to practice (or put into plan) once you have finished this book. Some may seem impossible, either to achieve or even start, but I ask of you only this: become aware, plan your next move, envision the success, take baby steps, keep at it, never give up, and, of course, believe in yourself.

Look for role models. If your parents were balanced in self-care and your care, then you could not have had better examples to prove that point. It could very well be that one of your parents was less into self-care than the other, but I want to refer to them as a unit. (The goal should be for parents to offer a balanced approach in partnership.) If you have had a wonderful childhood, then it's safe to assume that your parents were responsible, loving, considerate, and giving people while also ensuring that they nurtured their own well-being, values, and beliefs. On the other side of the spectrum, you may have observed your parents being completely selfless or too selfish, which most likely resulted in a more challenging environment growing up. They can be examples of what not to do.

For the most part, role models inspire us, we look up to them, and we want to be like them. They bring out our desire to be better, and they can fill our hearts and minds with aspirations of an achievable future. In addition, they make us feel great with their encouragement and support while empowering us to become empowered. Never miss an opportunity to hang out with your role models (or observe them). It may be surprising, but don't overlook children and adolescents as role models. They care about themselves naturally, and I often admire the passion they have for their somewhat egotistical and naive views on life. I think that's because they lack experience and a worldview; their sole focus is on themselves in the moment, without much thought given to the future or other people. Even so, there's some good selfishness in that behavior, and chances are, you could need some of that every now and then.

Financial freedom, or financial independence, is tremendously important, and I will mention it throughout most chapters. You may not think of it as self-care, but hear me out. Money (or lack thereof) impacts your lifestyle and your decisions. You must take care of your finances so that they don't own you. You, too, can get to financial freedom with focus and commitment. It will take time, but you will be able to obliterate a financial burden if you are willing to develop an action plan. More to come in the chapter about VALUE.

I was around fourteen or fifteen when I started working at a supermarket after school. Prior to that, I did get an allowance, but it was tiny. Nonetheless, my allowance was mine, and it gave me small liberties, such as buying candy, a new vinyl record (yes, I'm that old), or a soft drink when going out to a local youth meetup. I'm sure every child learns quickly that the more money there is, the more can be spent on things and activities one prefers. If I wanted out of my parent's house, I had to save up enough and/or earn enough to afford my own apartment and lifestyle. Fortunately, thanks to my frugal parents, my lifestyle was very affordable. Once I felt that I had achieved a certain level of independence at eighteen, I moved out, and I went pretty far. At seventeen, I had met a U.S. soldier, gotten married within a year, and moved from Germany to South Carolina. My certain level of "independence" was an alcoholic and jealous husband who had taken over my life and all decisions in it. Just like that, I was on my way to utterly fail at taking care of myself. I masked my unhappiness with material items, and so did my husband in his struggles to combat his divorced parents' repeated statements that he was unworthy because he reminded each of them of the other's bad traits. We took on a lot of debt together while drifting further and further apart. I felt trapped financially, and I tried to overcompensate by going into full denial mode. My goal was to keep up the visuals in front of everyone while also ignoring his mental and verbal abuse. I hid my misery, the financial and wedded one, from my family and friends because they had warned me, and I did not want them to be right, which meant that I had failed.

Financial independence can be tough to achieve whether you are single or married. However, it can be extremely complicated when your partner or spouse keeps overextending your credit. Then the challenge is not just putting a damper on spending while trying to pay off the mountain of debt, but it is also about having to convince another person—who may not share your viewpoint—to buy into a different lifestyle or image. What would it take for this other person to get on board? You cannot fight the financial battle alone, so it is crucial to talk to your partner/spouse about it to create a plan of action together. Bankruptcy can be a viable option, but it comes with consequences that can impact one's life for seven to ten years (bad credit rating, higher interest rates on loans, higher insurance premiums, and even rejection when applying for loans or jobs). Consider which option is worse (staying in debt and struggling or working with your debtors through a bankruptcy), and keep in mind that your credit rating may already be in the dumps if your debt-to-income ratio is off and/or you have been delinquent on bills. Bankruptcy can save you financially if you make a plan to rebuild afterwards, which means that you cannot repeat the behavior that got you there.

There certainly are ways to get out of debt. None of them are easy, but why would they be? Debt helps to keep people oppressed while empowering those who make huge profits off the interest alone. Even when your debt is small and/or manageable, anything you can do to improve your financial situation (pay off loans early, open an IRA or high-yield savings account, contribute to a 401[k]) will offer a huge return on the investment later.

Give some thought to your financial goals. Financial independence is important as it allows you the freedom of choice once achieved.

Live within your means. This is part of being financially independent. I always get tickled when I stream episodes of people looking for new houses and they comment how small the bedroom is or how there aren't enough bedrooms for all their friends and family to come visit. Are you really willing to spend so much more money and interest every month for the next thirty years in the hope or anticipation that your friends and family members will come stay with you? Think about the added cost that comes with houseguests (food, utilities, work, stress). Are you inviting them because you love having them around or because you are trying to show off how successful you are? A big house isn't necessarily the best idea. There are monthly expenses and upkeep that will limit you in other areas if you buy into the size expectation. Consider what you need, what may be a nice add-on, and what is just plain unnecessary. Also consider your larger goals in life. How will an overextension of credit or expenses impact your chances for success? Honestly determine what is important to you that is sustainable in the moment and in the future. Your life will be less stressful knowing that you can maintain your standard of living.

Save money for an emergency. You will sleep easier knowing that you'd be okay for a bit if things went sour. A good goal is to save enough money to last for about two months, which would buy you some breathing room should you become unemployed. We can make some bad decisions when we are struggling financially, not to mention the stress over having to keep up our financial obligations. Also keep in mind that if you were to lose your job, the absence of a buffer would leave you vulnerable to having to accept the next best employment offer. You don't want to be desperate, which could lead you to another situation where your employer owns you and exerts that power because they will know that you depend on that job. They may take advantage of you.

Self-indulge! You heard me. Do what you want to do when you want to do it. You don't need justification. As women, we often wait to treat ourselves. We do not think we are worthy of indulgence unless it is a reward for something, like an accomplished task or unpleasantries that we have been procrastinating on. Why wait? You deserve self-care without an occasion or reason (other than to self-care). Discover who you are, relax, read a book, do a puzzle, buy that treat, visit a friend, get a massage, go on vacation, be selfish (but stay within your means). Do what is good for your soul. Put yourself first. Don't dare to back out of planned you time, and do not feel guilty for being selfish. That will ruin the experience and defeat the purpose. Stop looking for reasons to justify (or excuse) it. You're only arguing with yourself. Do not care what others think. That's on them. Feel powerful in your decision and own it. Don't let others own your feelings. You must learn to prioritize your needs and wants above others at times. More on that later.

Be alone. And let me clarify that I don't mean being alone as in single. Being single, by the way (btw), should never be viewed as a negative. There's such a misconception that single people aren't happy. I would argue that most happy people are so because they like themselves no matter what their relationship status is. They have spent time learning about themselves, and they are authentic and confident in who they are and what they represent. So go ahead, spend some quality time with yourself and explore your thoughts. Sit with them and let them go where they want or need to go. I get that it can be scary. But why is that? Consider what you are trying to avoid. What are you worried about? What do you fear?

My hope is that this book will help you to face yourself and the scary intentional dedication to being alone with your thoughts, dreams, and fears. Maybe use the self-indulge suggestion for starters. Do something positive but make the action something that forces you to be by yourself, away from people. Maybe this can be a hike, a bike tour, or an activity that will also get the endorphins going to make you feel good. When you're in a positive setting (physically and mentally), it will be easier to process thoughts that can be scary or overwhelming otherwise.

Don't apologize! Women are great at apologizing, and it needs to stop. I'm not saying don't apologize when you make a mistake, definitely own up to it. I'm talking about the innate need for women to accept blame for everything. Or when women feel bad about having to give bad news. For example, when we can't make meetings or other proposed appointments, we tend to start our replies with, "I'm sorry," and then we immediately dive into an explanation on why we can't make it. Stop it! You do not owe anyone an explanation on why you can or cannot make a meeting. Simply state you can't and propose an alternate date without any explanation. Why would you offer more details than necessary? Does that other person care? What value would your explanation offer? Similarly, practice not using fillers or emotional phrases in your professional emails such as, "I feel that . . . I think . . . I believe . . ." Especially if you are in a leadership position. Feel, think, and believe are not strong terms to use to show you know what you're doing. It leaves room for someone to question what you are stating. Use facts—not emotions that sugarcoat or deflect. It makes you look weak and indecisive.

Set up boundaries, a.k.a. saying no! Another tough one for a lot of women. We want to please to a fault. If you are too busy for additional work, for example, why volunteer or accept it? I'm not saying don't be helpful, but really consider what that extra work would mean for you (and who is asking). Longer work schedules, less time with family, more stress, less sleep. What is the long-term consequence if you continually accept more and more? And consider if there will be a stopping point unless you set it. Sometimes you offer a hand, and they will take your sanity.

In leadership positions, it is vital that you learn to delegate and set limits. If you are promoted from within, it can be extremely difficult to reset the boundaries for your superiors and peers. If you are given work that is administrative, then you should no longer be doing admin work as a boss. You should be managing and delegating. The respect level must be reestablished with new parameters for you to succeed. Some of your peers will detest your new title or authority, and they will try to bully or intimidate you to test your strength and confidence. You must clearly define the new parameters to them and live and breathe them. It's not about being arrogant or rude but about setting yourself up for success in an assertive way. People will respect boundaries if you adhere to them yourself. In any direction. Bottom line: Don't let people walk all over you because they mistake your kindness for weakness.

Do not avoid confrontation. I used to hate confrontation. Confrontation is uncomfortable for most everyone. It has such a bad reputation. However, when I was in quality management, confronting the negatives and working toward solutions showed me the benefits of addressing issues quickly. Confrontation can deal with personal and professional differences, misunderstandings, negotiations, quality/service issues, etc. Confrontation is not about being mean or dishing out blame. It should always be about addressing an issue and working out a solution. We must start looking at confrontation as a positive to improve on something or someone. Think about it. When we let something fester, does it usually make the situation better or worse? Exactly. Now, it's important how we go about it. Any confrontation should involve honest facts and voicing our concerns with the simple goal of understanding where each party is coming from (also emotionally). Nonetheless, emotions cannot override facts or the purpose of wanting to make things better. If someone is hitting a sensitive spot, acknowledge it, and then figure out the reason why. Can you explain your emotion? Is it shame? Guilt? Could it stem from something in your past? There's nothing wrong with feeling bad. For a little while. Just don't get stuck in that feeling of guilt or shame.

Working in quality management and investigating root causes have helped me immensely in my drive to continually improve everything. And to look at all avenues honestly. With this book, you will be able to look at confrontations as interactions that can be steered to positive outcomes.

Avoid the blame game and **forgive yourself.** This is not the same as our constant need to apologize. Women hold on to a lot of things, such as bad memories, false hope, guilt, humiliation, and blame. (Self) blame ranks at the top. Of course, our society has contributed to this problem, and it is counting on women to keep accepting the blame to keep women in their place. Blame is a great tool for oppression, and here is a harsh example: When a woman is raped or assaulted, some people may point toward her provocative clothes or behavior. She must have either done something to invite the aggressor or wasn't paying enough attention to prevent it from happening. When the victim can be blamed, it means that the oppressor gets assigned less responsibility for their action, which means less of a burden to the patriarchal system in addressing or correcting the root cause. When you're being told repeatedly that everything that impacts you is your fault, then all your decisions and actions can become questionable. You start believing that anytime something bad happens (to you), you should have known better or done something differently than what you did. It permeates into all aspects of your daily life, including your mistakes. I'm no exception. When I make a mistake, I can really hold a grudge against myself. I tend to relive my mistake as if in self-punishment, a type of purgatory that I think I deserve. That's not healthy. I have come to appreciate that mistakes are opportunities to learn from and to improve on; they are not opportunities to assign blame. If we can accept mistakes as opportunities while also realizing that everyone makes mistakes, then we can make peace with them and let go of blame.

You must also forgive yourself. Forgiving is not forgetting. Not forgetting will help you not make that mistake again. Forgiving is accepting the fact that to err is human. Ask yourself why you don't want to let go. Why do you want to continue to punish yourself? Do you think so little of yourself? Do you believe others are perfect?

Here's an awesome tool I use for my screwups. I ask myself one question: "Will the world still turn tomorrow because I made a mistake?" Duh, of course it will. The sun will come up as well. In the grand scheme of things, how bad is your mistake? Especially at work. It's just work. Sure, someone may be uncomfortable or mad, a part may not arrive in time, or you set off the sprinkler system by running your forklift into it. So what? It is not important. Unless someone died, life goes on. Get over yourself thinking that your mistake is such a big deal.

Don't take it personally. In addition to blaming ourselves and apologizing profusely, we also tend to see everything and everyone as a personal attack on our integrity and character. Sure, some people interact with you a certain way because they want to affect you personally, but I would dare to say that most of them do not want to do you personal harm. When you take things personally, it most likely means that you have insecurities that another person has uncovered and is now unintentionally exploiting. That's on you, not them. Avoid assigning blame and move on.

There's something else to consider, and I used to be guilty of this: Do not read something (intent, accusation, feeling) into an action that isn't there. For example, when I worked in quality, I would occasionally receive emails from customers complaining about a potential defect. I would view these "accusations" as a personal attack on my integrity (and the work that my team had put into the product). I would let my emotions get the better of me, and I would only see the negatives and/or what I perceived the customer to have meant to have said. Often, I would fire back an instant reply, deflecting and ignoring the facts and the customer's concern, only to realize later that I had taken everything out of context. I have learned to let such emails sit for hours after my first reading. Then, after I have calmed down, I go back to reread the email without all my defenses riled up. I can't tell you how many times I have seen the blatant difference in what was being said to what I had taken away from it initially.

You must learn to view things factually and objectively, also knowing what values are involved, to see why you feel attacked. The tools for that I will provide in this guide. The point is, don't make everyone an enemy from the get-go. It takes too much energy while not offering a return on your investment.

Be honest. It always is the best foot forward. The best part is that there are no lies that need to be remembered or upheld. I have quite the reputation among my friends for being honest. In a personal setting, I don't necessarily volunteer my observations or thoughts, but when asked, I call it. I don't try to avoid the negatives either. When my friends want an honest opinion, they know that they can rely on me to give them that honesty that they seek. I would dare to state that it's one of the things my friends value the most about me, even when it hurts their feelings at times. Again, I'm not a dick about it, but dishonesty will have larger and more impacting negative consequences and will result in people not trusting your words. One of my rules of honesty is that I would never say something about someone (not present) that I wouldn't say to their face. You know that others will gossip, so make it a point to stand by what you say. What and how you say something are important, and it matters. Honesty will force you to become a better communicator as it takes more practice and skill to remain factual in a way that doesn't offend.

The same approach applies in a professional setting, but here, I am not as reserved in dishing out my honest thoughts when it's a must and crucial to the business. My job as a business leader is not to appease my peers or superiors. I work for a company, and ultimately, if I am running a company (or a department), then I must look out for the interest of the company (which may not align with the interests of business owners or other superiors). That's where honesty is, honestly, difficult to represent at times, but there are legal, ethical, and social consequences if there aren't people who can protect businesses (and in turn, people working in them). Honesty results in a clean conscience.

Object, a.k.a. make your voice be heard. As referred to in the previous paragraph, sometimes we do not agree with others and/or we doubt their intentions and ambitions. It is important not to remain silent, especially if whatever you are objecting against could cause harm, be dangerous, unethical, illegal, inconsiderate, etc. Our silence at times can be empowering to the oppressors. If you don't feel comfortable in any scenario (someone talks rudely about you or others, someone asks you to do something that you can't or won't do, someone is insensitive to the needs of others), then it's okay to express that in a way that is not offensive or insulting. "I'm not comfortable with XYZ," works in any scenario, which may warrant further explanation. That explanation must be based on facts and/or concerns rooted in facts.

At work, you may need to involve the HR department, asking to witness your objection and/or to take down a written statement to be made part of your personnel file. You could also object via email if there is no HR or if the "offender" is a customer, vendor, or third party. Naturally, you must be factual and non-offensive (unemotional). If you are really upset, write your email, save it as a draft, and then open it again after several hours. Reread it, and then take out all the emotions that have surely found their way in. This would include sentences that include words like *feel, think, believe, fear*. Present facts in a polite way without insult. I really love this approach. My first draft often includes many intentional puns and accusations because it feels great writing it down as an acknowledgment of my disgust. In my rewrite later, I often chuckle at my obvious emotional undertone, and then I rephrase my sentences to show professionalism and composure while being on point factually. This method allows me to remain objective in my objection without adding insult to injury.

Making your objection part of a record can protect you when things turn ugly later.

Keep your dreams or ambitions top of mind. Too often, we settle for less because it may be the better or more practical path (financially or emotionally). We have the best intentions to get back on track in the pursuit of our dreams. Then we forget or ignore what we once held so highly in our sights. Call it complacency that doesn't really satisfy. It's very important to keep pursuing your dreams no matter what happens. You can only push your priorities down for so long before it drains your energy and motivation. It is also okay to acknowledge that our dreams can change while we have them on the back burner. In five years from now, I will be in a different spot, I will have changed, and my goals may not be the same anymore. You can pivot at any time. The mistake would be to hold on to something that you are no longer passionate about but feel that you should still pursue because you have said so.

Of course, life happens while we make our plans. Unplanned things do happen, and you may need to pivot everything due to unforeseen reasons (such as a death in the family or a sickness, a job loss, etc.). Do what is necessary to get through whatever is stopping you now, but do not lose sight.

One word on major crises: We all experience them, and we must adapt to make it through. However, if you find yourself stumbling from one fiasco to the next, then you must step back to evaluate (and value) your life. There must be a cycle there that needs to be broken. I always wondered how some people are always stuck in crisis mode without ever having or making a plan B or C. While bad things happen, we can be prepared for some things or at least expect something (bad) to happen. Most of the time, a prolonged series of crises stems from financial dependence, unrealistic time management skills, and selective procrastination that prevents one to deal with issues before or as they arise.

Nourish your faith. I'm not a religious person, but faith does not necessarily have to come from religion. Nonetheless, religion is everything to a lot of people, and besides the spiritual benefits, it also offers a community, and with it, an awesome support system. In a nonreligious context, having faith means that you believe in or can count on something that is or is not a tangible. We can have faith in something like a skill or a characteristic.

I have faith. I have learned that I can always count on my resilience, adaptiveness, and smarts to get me through (and so much more). The way I nourish my faith is by continuing the learning process in fun ways (crosswords, puzzles, riddles, personality tests, hobbies) in addition to more conventional learning (reading, taking classes, etc.). There are tangibles to get to the intangibles. My faith in a sense is all of me, in my entirety, and me acknowledging who I am (and loving me).

Self-care sustains my faith (my belief in myself). It's that simple. Find what you believe in. Redefine faith into something that is more real than make-believe, and then nourish it so you can draw strength from it.

Focus on your health. This includes a good diet, adequate hydration, restful sleep, some type of exercise, and mental awareness. Sometimes you cannot appreciate good health until you lose it. I want you to turn that focus around so that you can learn your health based on a healthy state versus waiting for it to decline where you are trying to regain that feeling of health. Acknowledge each day how you feel inside and out, and this will establish your health baseline. If you do that, then it will become easier to notice when you are wearing down, and you can take steps quicker to recover.

If you are not practicing a healthy lifestyle, you are missing out. I'm not talking about crazy diets (or any diet). I'm talking about a balance in food choices, coupled with some type of physical activity at a level that makes you feel good and that you can maintain. It is not super complicated to make smarter food choices, and you do not have to be rich either. The only thing you need is honesty, and the only person you are trying to deceive is yourself when you make excuses for why you are not acting on your intentions. Making conscious decisions about what you put in your body and then following through are two different things.

My kryptonite is jalapeno (or most all flavored) potato chips. Give me the entire bag and I could eat every last crumb. I'm honest about my behavior, and I don't practice avoidance. Why would I? I love potato chips. Instead, I've learned to pour my chips in a certain size container to avoid binging. Counting calories can give you a great idea of how much food you consume every day. I heard it takes 3,500 extra calories a week for you to gain a pound. It sounds like a lot, but when you start tracking calories (for your body type), then it quickly becomes crystal clear that we typically exceed our allowed count on a daily basis.

Food affects you, and it either gives you a benefit or it causes a drawback, physically and emotionally. The damage emotionally can be worse because you may feel that nothing you do physically (in your perception of countering those calories) helps shed those extra pounds. The older you get, the harder this becomes as our metabolisms change dramatically with age. I'm not immune to it. I realize I have to be more active while eating less of the wrong things just to maintain. I've committed to doing that. When I fall off that jalapeno-chip wagon occasionally, I don't beat myself up over it. Falling off is the exception, not the rule.

If you are neglecting yourself in this important pillar of self-care, then everything becomes much harder when it doesn't have to be like that. It is one of the easiest areas of your life to take charge of, but it requires commitment and dedication as the beginning will suck. And I said "easiest" only because it is the most obvious. It definitely is not easy to do. However, you will find that taking charge of yourself and your health will help empower you to achieve other goals. The downside is, if you make a half-ass effort and fail, your other goals may also become unachievable in your mind. Deep down, you know all this to be true. You must face your inner asshole if you want to succeed at eating healthier. What is the real reason you are not committing to a better version of yourself? Be honest, acknowledge, and do not get lost in shame or self-pity. Now is the time to start small. Change just one bad food habit into a viable and sustainable success story.

The benefits of good eating and exercising habits are huge. You will gain energy, endorphins will kick in, and your brain will process everything better, and you will feel accomplished. Take baby steps in the right direction.

Do not overlook meditation or yoga to balance out the stresses in your life. Being centered and focusing on mindfulness will do wonders for your overall well-being.

Go to therapy. When you get really stuck in life, it's best to seek professional help. Talking with a therapist can often be the best avenue when you struggle deeply with your emotions or memories—or life in general. That objective view from a stranger will allow you to open up with more honesty and without judgment that you may expect from, let's say, a good friend. There's no relationship to protect when dealing with a therapist.

Having said that, sometimes your best friend could be a proxy therapist. It depends on your relationship and how severe or unmanageable your problem is. If you can be truly honest with your bestie, and you value each other deeply and with respect (after spilling your darkest secrets), then this could be your ticket. Nevertheless, for those prolonged crises and/or deep emotional traumas, you will be better served by a professional therapist who has more tools in their toolbox to offer solutions that may work for you. If you cannot afford therapy, see if there are any support groups or local meetups in your area where you can meet people in similar situations. There's still some anonymity in these group settings while allowing for emotions and fears to surface in a safe environment. You may come across a counselor who could also get you to the right support if the group sessions are not helping.

The goal is not to fester on bad feelings or thoughts. You must find an outlet that works for you to acknowledge what's happening on your inside if you want to move forward with your life.

Hang out with your tribe. There's nothing more uplifting than being around your friends who can take care of your emotional needs. They know how you tick, your likes, dislikes, and they love you for who you are. Spending time with them is good for your soul. They are your safe zone. Relationships matter. And the simple fact that you can be yourself without any pretenses or expectations is priceless. I bet your friends will be there for you in whatever capacity you need them to be. Say, "Distract me," when you just want to be in a moment without the heaviness of your day, or, "Do you have a minute for me?" when you need someone to talk to. Ask and you shall receive. Your tribe will give you energy and purpose.

A word of caution: Give some thought to the size of your tribe. In a recent conversation with one of my best friends, he said that he feels that he should make an effort to be friends with everyone who wants to be his friend. I can tell you that this would be an impossible task. Everyone he meets wants to be friends with him. He's that awesome. He has that aura that draws people in. He's a great listener and communicator, and he always seems to have the right words, actions, ideas, thoughts. He simply is in tune with each of his friends, effortlessly I had assumed. However, in our talk, I realized that he puts a huge amount of energy and time into maintaining and cultivating his relationships. I mean ALL of them. He was stressing over how and when to nurture those relationships, and he worried about how to manage the load if he were to add more friendships. Think about it. Anytime he meets new people, he can feel anxious about having to make more friends that he does not want to disappoint. Wow. I don't even have words for this selflessness, other than, don't lose yourself in your tribe. If quality is important, then it cannot come at the cost of quantity. Don't spread yourself too thin. Instead of friends, some people can be acquaintances. It doesn't take away from your feelings for them (or vice versa). Either way, in a nutshell, though, none of your friends or acquaintances have any expectation of you regarding frequency and time spent together. Not if those people are your true friends.

Get enough sleep. I'm very cranky when I don't get eight hours of good sleep. Do you know what your number is? Our bodies need rest, and so does the brain. It is important to let ourselves recover from the day. Avoid looking at your phone before bedtime because it will only rile you up, and most likely, lead you down a rabbit hole of social media engagement that will prevent you from hitting the sack. The same goes for TV. It's best to avoid watching anything upsetting before going to bed. My sleep is impacted by what I hold on to in my thoughts when my head hits the pillow. Try some breathing techniques or meditation to calm your inner voices just before bedtime.

I also take naps when I notice I'm wearing down. It is not uncommon for me to lie down on the couch in the afternoon for some rest. I've never been one to have an abundance of energy. Things and people deplete my energy quickly, and I know myself well enough to realize that for me to recharge, I need to disengage. When I take naps, I also cannot just do a quickie. My naps are at least an hour, sometimes longer. While you cannot nap at work, you can still be conscious of your energy levels. Take a quick break, go for a walk during lunch, or hide in the bathroom for a few quiet minutes if it helps recharge you. Consider how you need energy to interact for your benefit. Don't let your battery run dry. I have and love my fitness watch, which tells me about my sleep cycles, stress levels, and body battery. It is not always correct, but it can be a good aid in understanding my body as it relates to stress and different environments.

Give a compliment to a friend or a stranger. Seeing them smile or perk up will make you feel great. That compliment can also change someone's day or outlook on life. We put so much value on the beauty that someone else sees, so be an advocate for kindness and joy. I bet, the more frequently we compliment, the greater the ripple effect. Why do we refrain from telling people something nice? I don't know either, so do it.

Here's the deal with compliments, and it is the reason I categorize them as self-care: They are positive affirmations that will help you see the beauty in everything, including yourself. I would like to challenge you to observe someone and to only note something positive—even if there's a negative screaming at you. What were your eyes drawn to first? Be honest. Do you find yourself mostly noticing uncomplimentary things? Do you typically resort to putting people down when observing from afar? I was guilty of that. Still can be. Especially when everyone has beaten you down, it is hard to see something nice in others because we feel that it confirms that they are better than us. I know it sounds crazy and ugly. But don't overlook that, for women, it is hard to see something positive in others that we would rather have discovered in ourselves. Sometimes, I simply assume that the other person has had an easy life, things were handed to them, and it allows me to be hateful in my observations about that person. It's sad, but it doesn't make me a hateful person. I'm a child of my environment and my experiences. It means that I had to fight for a lot, and I feel that I have not gotten the recognition I deserve. Sound familiar?

When you can start forcing yourself to see the good things in people, it will reinforce your thoughts into a pattern of shutting out the negatives. Or at least you are aware of your typical pattern of negativity, and then you can turn off the bad thoughts. Seeing the positives and giving compliments will manifest positivity. It's really depressing (and not pretty) looking at everything with negativity, so let's get busy handing out those compliments. Start with yourself.

At first glance, this next item may not seem like self-care, but I want to list it because survival can be a form of self-preservation, and therefore, self-care. **Protect yourself from traumatic emotional stresses.** With this, I mean existential threats. A lot of people cannot relate to this situation. But there will be those of us who have lived and survived abuse that could have threatened our lives. If you are currently in such a toxic relationship, then you know that emotional protection (on both sides) is critical when dealing with abusive personalities. You must try to avoid pushing your abuser into a corner where they retaliate with violence or other forms of abuse. Their emotional protection in this sense means their safe zone, as in unprovoked (their normal emotional state). You will be familiar with how to maintain the (in)sanity, and it will protect you from experiencing those intensity-gaining emotional stresses. When surrounded by many triggers (also the weapon kind), it is important to walk on eggshells until you can get out.

Know this: You are never truly alone, and you can find help in many places without alerting the abuser. Churches, support groups, medical professionals, friends, women's organizations, etc. are all avenues available to you when wanting to leave an abusive relationship. Many women have walked that path before you. Be timely and smart in stepping off that path before it leads to your doom. It is that serious.

Let's talk about the people who misunderstand self-care. These people do everything for their own benefit without empathy or sympathy toward others. They are selfish in the worst way (they may be the reason you are reading this book). They are the abusers, the hateful, the bad bosses, the evil managers, the mean relatives, the bullies. They are aggressive and defensive at the same time. Like babies that have grown into adults: crying loudly, demanding your empathy, your sympathy, your dignity. Those selfish beings will suck out your energy and rob you of everything that's valuable to you. And the more empowered you become, the louder they will cry. They have suffered more, they are being punished, they are being treated unfairly, the world is against them, yet somehow, their privileged selves will demand your constant worship and attention.

That is not the selfish we want. But it confirms that there are always two ways of approaching something. You need to be conscious about the choices made—there's a good and a bad selfishness. Self-care is a (good) selfish act, and its purpose is for the betterment of everyone, starting with yourself.

Taking care of yourself as a life skill means being able to live by yourself and being able to afford all the expenses that come with that independence, alongside the physical, mental, and emotional capacity to be a functional and thriving citizen so that you can also support your fellow human beings. If you have a spouse, children, or animals, then everything becomes a bit more complex, but the principle remains the same.

Taking Care of Others

Societies cannot survive without taking care of their citizens. Societies must help most everyone, and they must benefit most everyone to work properly. Taxes serve that purpose as do social programs resulting from such taxes or fees (school, social security, etc.), and we all benefit as a society. The same applies to people within societies. People in communities (and tribes) must depend on each other while supporting each other to sustain.

As an individual, if you don't learn how to take care of yourself first, you will be less successful at taking care of others! You can attempt, and you will struggle. Unless you are selfish, you will not be able to sustain your physical and mental health. Think about it. You cannot build on a foundation that is weak, has no structure, no support, no base. Your foundation is your strength, your smarts, your heart, your brain. You will collapse eventually if you are adding what ultimately is too much to sustain.

Selfishness is underrated. As we Southerners like to state, "You can try to grow vegetables in clay, but in the end, clay just sticks to your shoes when it rains." Not sure where I came up with that, but you must be good to clay, improve on it, mix in some good soil, and then water it appropriately.

Selfishness is always about taking care of yourself FIRST. That's the basis that we will use to take care of others.

How Do We Take Care of Others?

Be a role model. We show others that we can take care of ourselves first. They will learn from our example. We want to be the light that someone else sees in the dark.

Be kind, a.k.a. don't be a dick! That should be rule number one in any scenario. Be a decent human being and be compassionate to all living things. Try not to be judgmental. Approach everyone with an open heart, open eyes, and most importantly, an open mind. Nod a greeting, give a compliment, open the door for someone, smile. Block out any negativity and stop pretending to be oblivious to other people's struggles when it is obvious. Being kind should be one of the easiest things. But in today's world, it can be difficult not to let the negativity impact our mood and behavior. Try to become aware of what you are exposed to every day. Can you determine the positive and negative influencers? Do you think you can impact change in that regard? I bet you can be kind(er) with a bit more effort.

Show up. Be available, reachable, approachable while not being judgmental at the same time. Offering a shoulder to cry on and listening are two of the most effective ways to take care of others. It's that simple. Sure, you can give advice and offer honesty without being insulting, but sometimes, just sitting with a friend in silence is good enough. Show that you care, assure that mistakes happen to everyone, point toward a path forward, and do not dwell on regrets or blame.

The other day, I spoke to a close friend whom I value immensely. We talked about the depths of friendships and about being there for one another. I mentioned that I had felt guilty because I had not been a very present friend when his partner died of a prolonged illness. I had wondered if my friend ever considered me to have been a bad friend. He hadn't. We agreed that there isn't a right or wrong amount of showing up. I'm sure you've seen movies where friends put their entire worlds on hold to be there for their besties in times of need. That is not the expectation of your friends, trust me. We all have jobs, families, and our own plate of sorrows. Showing up for your friends does not require you to live up to the expectation set by a movie. You can be as present as you can be under your current circumstances. And, btw, you should also ask your friends what level of showing up they want. They may not want you there all the time, and they will appreciate you asking.

A word of caution: Beware of those individuals who mistake support for the opportunity to rant about nonsensical issues, spread lies, or act hateful. We show up to encourage acceptance and change, not to add fuel to a fire or to encourage verbal vomit. Listen with intent to recognize the difference. If all you ever hear is self-validation, self-pity, or trash talk to an unacceptable degree, shut your ears and discontinue that toxic relationship before it becomes unhealthy to your self-care.

Other times, you are dealing with true victims though. They feel terribly stuck in their situation, and they are too afraid to initiate change or ask for help. They will deflect or ignore any feedback or advice when you try to softly approach them. Ultimatums will never work and can result in you losing that friend, which would only add more stress to their already almost unmanageable lives. All you can do is be present and consistent (and nonjudgmental). That's enough. You want to be the light they see when they are ready.

Be a mentor who is approachable. If you are good at what you do, then others will admire you. They may want to learn from the best (yes, you). Never view anyone as competition or out to get your job. That would mean that you have no confidence in your abilities. Or it could mean that your company does not see your value. Doesn't matter though. Mentorship is about empowering others. It's not about protecting your knowledge for fear of being left behind. If that is the case, then there are deeper issues at play, and your job may not be the most beneficial to you.

As a mentor, give your students the tools that will help them succeed and thrive. Their success is your success. Additionally, their empowerment will relieve you of some of the more mundane types of work while allowing you to focus on bigger projects. Mentorship is a win-win in most environments.

Being a mentor also results in learning from the other person and in forming social bonds and allies. Your students will go out into the world, and they will remember you as a mentor who was willing to share and empower. This will expand your network as well as your reputation. Never assume that you don't know enough to be a mentor. Mentorship is also about life experiences and values. You have all of that.

Donate. When you consider donations, it could be in the form of time, money, or material items. There are so many organizations looking for support with any of those options. Pick one that represents an issue close to your heart, and you will find that you will get so much in return.

The easiest donations will be materialistic items that may no longer have a value to you, but that could make a huge difference in someone else's life. Give unused, unnecessary items a second purpose. Donate clothes to a homeless shelter. Take your old TV to Goodwill. Pick up some food to give to a homeless person in your area, or see if instead of food, clothing or shoes may be better options depending on the climate.

If you do not have things or money to donate, then time is your most precious gift. Some organizations may prefer volunteers who are willing to show up versus those making a materialistic or financial contribution. When you can be at the front lines helping those who need more help than yourself, you may even get the biggest return on your investment on an emotional level. Be respectful while not being judgmental. Unconditional love is best, and it will be received in honesty. Volunteering your time can truly show you what a positive impact you can have in an instant. Most Americans are only a few paychecks away from being bankrupt or homeless. Never assume it could never happen to you. Appreciate what you have and pay it forward when you are able.

Let's talk about financial support. My advice is to be careful when to give it and how. There are so many other ways to take care of others first. As an example, that homeless person begging at that intersection, hand them food or drink items versus cash. You are not going to make a difference in getting them a home by dropping some change into their hands. Why not ask that person what they need? Maybe they need new shoes, a warm sweater, something tangible that you can then purchase and bring to them. Offer them info on shelters or food pantries. If they don't want any of what you're offering, that's on them.

You should never feel obligated to give money. Even when someone asks or begs. I'm not saying don't give money. But be careful and conscious about the guilt factor in your decision. Is it guilt because you have an easy life compared to the asker and you want to give because you feel it's the right thing to do? Or is it because they make you feel guilty in how they approach the ask?

The point is that guilt and fear are used way too frequently to pressure someone into giving money. As stated earlier, people can be selfish in the wrong way. You have the option and right to say no to someone asking for money without feeling guilty about how the other person feels about your response. You are not responsible for their feelings (or their circumstances). There are struggles you have overcome yourself to get to where you are. You earned and deserve what you have.

Having said that, it is your prerogative to extend financial aid. It's totally okay to give without prejudice, expectations, or strings attached. In fact, I would encourage you to expect nothing from giving money other than to feel good. You cannot spend hours wondering what that person did with YOUR money. Once it leaves your hands, it's no longer yours to decide over. Make peace with that. If we are talking larger sums and familiar people, and you want to ensure the money goes to where it's needed, pay for someone's rent, power bill, groceries, etc., and make it a point to pay the vendor directly to ensure the money is going where it is needed. Consider exchanging services for money, like having your car washed every week in return for weekly support. However, just because you do this once does not translate into the expectation of you continuing the financial support indefinitely.

I'd advise against putting your name on someone else's loan unless it's someone you know and trust (and who is financially responsible). Our credit system determines your value as a consumer, which translates into your premiums for insurance and loans as well as your consideration for employment. Do not lose your financial freedom to an abuser of your kindness.

From providing financial and emotional support to offering a place to live, to babysit, to mow a lawn, to donating . . . there's too many to list, but in summary, taking care of others is simply the fact that we can be there in whatever capacity we can offer when needed for the right reasons—without damaging self-care long-term.

Sometimes, we don't have a choice. Having to take care of others can happen unexpectedly. You may have a family member with a life-altering medical prognosis, and they will need personal care, financial help, etc. We have and/or feel an obligation to help, especially when it's family, but our obligation should not come at the expense of our financial independence or emotional stability.

My suggestion is to be time/goal limited when giving all of yourself to care for someone else. Commit to finding times and places to decompress and to nourish your faith. Remember, the expectation is not to do it all for others while forsaking yourself. Create a support system to alleviate some of the burden. We all go through rough times when our chips are down, but you must not walk this path alone.

Let's talk about codependency. Codependency is when you abandon your own emotions and needs and you "give" yourself and everything in your power to someone who may abuse your kindness and concern. Codependency is a relationship addiction (because you lose yourself in that relationship that has taken over your life, yet it seems impossible to break away). Having said that, codependency can be at its worst when the relationship is between a parent and a child. Especially when that child spirals out of control. What should you, could you do? You want to do everything in your power to help. The love and connection you feel to your child are irreplaceable. I cannot relate as I do not have children. The best advice I can give is still the same: You cannot take care of others if you lose yourself in them. You can be there, but there is a fine line between enablement and emotional support. You must learn the difference, and I would encourage you to read up on codependency.

In that same breath, you must realize that not everyone wants to be taken care of. Think of the earlier example I gave where my sister baked treats despite my stern wish for her not to go through the trouble. Though in that instance, we are not talking about existential or essential help that would aid in anyone's survival. Yet, even when someone is in dire need of help (to self-sustain/survive), the scenario could be the same. That person may not want your help. You cannot force someone to accept help. Well, not accurate, I know, but if you do, there is no honesty. You can't change or make someone change on a deeper level without honesty to see and accept things for the way they are. Even when they do, they may prefer to stay in the dark. Don't get lost with them but offer to be the light when they are ready.

If you know how to be selfish, it's much easier to spot the right timing. Chances are, if you are not selfish, you'll lose yourself in the other person's misery just like I had done with my drunkard. If I had been selfish, I would have never let him treat me the way he did. I would have seen my value.

This about sums up the learning life skills. Time to dig deeper into what learning means to us and why it is so important.

Learning Is Knowledge

Knowledge will give you confidence and empowerment. You can represent the topics that you are passionate about with facts and conviction. Some people confuse knowledge with information or opinion, and they will stand by their viewpoints no matter how factually inaccurate. There is so much disinformation out there (social media especially), and it threatens our lives, our democracy, our freedom, our laws. I never understood how ignorant people can argue over fake news. They must be too lazy to learn. It's much easier to watch from the sidelines, not aware of where information is coming from. If you tell a lie over and over, eventually it becomes the truth. Sad fact.

How Do We Learn?

The first thing that comes to mind is **school**. A country's educational system has a lot to do with the culture and the fabric of its society. I am blessed that I received my education in Germany, a country with a great educational system and many valuable social programs. While the United States (still) is a democratic country, the basic educational system (at least in the South) is one of exclusion and limitations. Spending five years in South Carolina, tutoring a relative, made me see how the government wants to keep certain people uneducated. The less they know, the better followers they are. The less they will question. They can be kept down low to maintain the status quo of oppression.

To me, there also seems to be too many variables and distractions in the American school system and not enough subjects on or opportunities for critical thinking. I often wonder how parents do it with their children participating in so many after-school activities. Learning is hard with all the distractions outside of school. Learning too much about social expectations and nothing about critical thinking helps the government in developing followers. Additionally, without critical thought and discussions, many subjects are not taught fully and properly. The absence of something can say a lot about the intention of the governing body. If teachers question that themselves, they get punished. Some schools have hotlines to report teachers who try to be more inclusive in the curriculum. Books are lobbied against, even banned, because a privileged (white) person is not comfortable with the subject matter. Censorship is all about preventing you from learning something that could be a danger to the current system.

When it comes to school learning, we must go through the motions for the most part. Don't rely on what you learned in school to get you through life. If you are still reading, you are probably laughing. Old news recycled. We should not and cannot rely on the government to instill broader and inclusive knowledge. We must look to other sources to educate ourselves. Because learning is the ultimate investment in yourself.

Pursue further academic learning at any age. Attend college (in person or online). No doubt, college degrees will enable you to get to some things easier, such as certain jobs at certain companies, a higher salary, more book smarts, credibility in your studied field, added respect from certain groups, professional allies, and better critical thinking skills (through diversity and research options available at universities). College can be an awesome place to gain expert knowledge (specialized areas of interest or jobs), but it can also offer a protected space to discover yourself because the sole purpose and focus of college is, well, to learn. Another upside is that many different minds and mindsets converge at a university, offering other viewpoints, opinions, theories, and solutions. It's a great place to interact and to learn about life outside your bubble. I would imagine that the professors also facilitate great discussions while posing deep questions, encouraging critical thought, in a safe environment. Not to mention the books and other research papers that you would not easily have access to otherwise. College is an awesome place for learning without the distractions of an otherwise hectic life. The biggest downside is the cost, and for many people, college is not an option.

A more cost-effective alternative is community college. Pick up a curriculum, and you may be surprised at the offerings. You can learn a new skill or trade and take shorter classes on self-development, how to start a business, retirement planning, language learning, painting, etc. I've taken a motorcycle safety class and other one-day courses about leadership. From short- to long-term courses, you will find something of interest at your community college.

How about **e-learning**: streaming services (such as YouTube), online continuing education platforms, etc. If you want to figure out how to do something, chances are there's a video or a course somewhere online that will teach you. Some of these are made by people who aren't even real experts. Do your homework on who you trust to teach you. Not everyone needs to be an expert to teach something. YouTube is proof of that.

E-learning academic platforms are a great resource when it comes to many subject matters. A lot of their offered courses are free, and once signed up, you get to set your own schedule. No commitment to a daily routine or certain time block, but be aware that most courses must be completed within a certain timeframe from starting. If you see a price tag next to a course, look for the option without a certificate. You will be excluded from a few things, such as interactions with other students, tests, final exams, but it's all stuff that is not crucial.

While on my first sabbatical a few years ago, I took an online gender study class, and I loved it. Even though it only scratched the surface, it gave me a plethora of information to continue learning on my own once done with the course. Plus, it helped me with this book as well. No effort is ever wasted unless you let it be.

Your employer may offer continuing education or seminars. Always jump at an opportunity for personal development or learning a new skill, especially if your company is paying for it. Continuing education, in any shape or form, is instrumental in our learning ambitions for any career. Even when you are not interested in an offered seminar, I'd advise you to take it. Seminars are good places to meet other people (who work for different companies), so never turn down a chance to expand your network.

Mentors can be an alternative to academic learning (or an addition). You've certainly had mentors. Most of mine were men, which seems normal considering that the manufacturing world that I inhabited for over twenty-five years was (and is) full of male leaders. Finding women mentors in business can be tough. The world is so competitive for women, with so few seats at the table available to them. It makes us natural enemies.

Mentors can be experts at a trade, area of expertise, or skill. They take pride in their work, and they don't exclude or withhold. However, not all mentors are experts. Some are average people with an extraordinary sense of responsibility. Others simply have talent. I dare to say that all of them are hard workers with a purpose, and they care about quality and integrity. They inspire others to do and be better.

My chosen mentors were willing and happy to share their knowledge. They were smart enough to know that empowerment meant more support and free time for them. In my quest to throw myself into learning the things that I needed to learn, I heavily relied on my mentors, and I never pretended to know it all once I had reached top management. Mentors are needed throughout all levels. However, keep in mind that someone with a negative impact can also be a mentor; you will learn from them what not to do.

Read to educate or read for fun. You can read just about anything, anywhere. Reading is free when you sign up at a local library. You can also read online, in bookstores, on a tablet, laptop, phone, or you can exchange books with family and friends, subscribe to a paper or blog, etc. While learning is the purpose with educational or nonfiction books, keep in mind that even when reading for fun, the aim should be to learn something. You can accomplish this with any book, new or old, different or the same, out of your comfort zone or within. I encourage you to dive into experiences that are far removed from your environment, escape into fantasy or dystopian worlds, and lose yourself in that steamy romance. Whatever it is though, make it your goal to walk away with one newfound benefit or revelation. Put some thought behind what you are reading. Did the author have a purpose? Is there a message for you? Why did the writing speak to you? What did you feel and why?

Listen up. Another great learning option is through audiobooks and podcasts. Audio learning and listening are good fillers of time when your hands, eyes, or other body parts are otherwise occupied. Listen to an audiobook during your commute or dive into your favorite podcast. Pay attention to song lyrics, dial into your favorite radio station or program. Listen with purpose; there's always more to what's being said, and there can be interesting morsels to be discovered in how the words were spoken (tone, loudness, pitch).

How about listening to learn about your family history? How much do you really know about your parents, grandparents, great-great-parents? Typically, we don't know much past our parents' generation. And even with that, you barely have looked at your parents as people with dreams and ambitions. Maybe you have, and that would be awesome. Sit down with them, if you're still lucky enough to do so, and ask about their lives before you: how they met, where they worked, what they did for fun, what struggles they had to overcome, etc. You will be thankful to know your roots better. Knowing those roots will help you know yourself. Those conversations can then lead you down the road to pursuing local or global history, researching ancestors, traveling to a new country, learning how to play the bagpipe, etc.

Language learning offers so many insights. It's not just a way to communicate, but it also offers a view into a country's mentality, culture, inner social structures, and history. When you can realize that other countries use different words to describe something that makes no sense when translated into your native tongue, then you can start accepting the differences in cultures without prejudice. It allows you to take a pause when dealing with foreigners who may not speak English well.

If you were to learn Arabic for example, you would encounter a lot of topics in your pursuit of learning the language that would explain the culture and the mindset as well as the religion. Pay close attention to the way the grammar is constructed and how things are being said. It may sound crazy, but it's true. A lot can be lost in translation when we don't consider how the language is used in conveying feelings and beliefs or how certain words can describe things, places, moods, and even jokes that would make no sense in our own language.

This could be especially helpful when disagreeing with someone. A lot of our human problems are about cultural differences. If you can understand the reasoning behind the differences, it opens the door to communication. For example, it is easy to criminalize a person based on religion for any of their actions because of mainstream media's one-sided viewpoint. The word *Islam* is being used as a synonym for *terror*, and we simply are led to assume that all terrorists are Muslims and that all Muslims are terrorists. It's the same approach when Christians say that gay people won't go to heaven. Christians don't go to heaven because they are straight—or do they? Christians also don't go to heaven for merely calling themselves that.

Learning languages can be such an eye-opener to people's behaviors when you consider how the language (or culture) was formed and how some countries have different meanings for identical words or gestures. It teaches compassion and provides a bridge to better communications and interactions.

A **hobby** is about gaining knowledge. Have you always wanted to learn how to ride a horse? Rebuild a muscle car? Write a book? Level up in a video game? Swim like a mermaid? Run a marathon?

A hobby will teach you a lot about yourself. Mind you, though, be smart in your approach. It's best to find your tribe that can teach you holistically and ensure you have a good foundation. There's a journey of progression with most hobbies. Just like you can't strap on a parachute and jump out of an airplane, you can't gain knowledge without putting in some research, training, and effort first. Enjoy the journey and be safe about it.

Not every hobby will be free. Be honest about how much you can spend in what timeframe and be clear about the objective. Jogging will involve athletic wear and some good running shoes, but after that, it's all about adding luxury to the hobby, such as wireless earbuds, a fancy fitness tracking device, etc. Luxury items are nice-to-haves but not must-haves. You can run quite well without accessories if you don't have the budget.

I had always wanted to ride a horse. Not the cheapest hobby—it's a money pit really—but in my midtwenties, I went in with a small budget and pulled it off. Looking back, it was a big investment in my personal and professional growth, unintentionally at first, but then most hobbies will offer a huge return on the investment if you go in with your eyes and mind wide open.

Do you have a **talent**? Don't discount that having a talent for something can be an opportunity to learn. It may seem like a contradiction since people with talent are prone to do something well naturally. But even a talent could be honed by simply focusing on what can be improved upon or what it would take to step it up to the next level. However, never forget that talent is not about competition, and it doesn't mean that you are better than others. Talent is a learning gift that should not be wasted.

Human interactions will make you learn about, well, humans. While I understand that you are reading this book in order to have better interactions, let's acknowledge that interactions in general are great when evaluating others on behavior. I'm not saying actively throw yourself into more interactions. Observe them. There's so much to be learned from observing, and I will expand on this in the next chapter.

The point is to have and observe interactions in a safe environment. Hang out with people who share your interest(s), volunteer, join a political party, attend business seminars, or have a beer or wine social at your home or elsewhere with like-minded people. Whatever. Start your own group, meeting, or social event; find new ideas, expand your comfort zone, and build up your confidence.

If you want to challenge yourself, then you can try to get out of your comfort zone. Hang out with (or near) people who don't share your interest(s). Could be fun. Could be stressful. It probably will be both. Knowledge is also about what the other side thinks. Right or wrong, you cannot learn about something by just looking at it from one perspective. There are always two sides to each coin. My suggestion would be to remain very observant when hanging out with people outside of your tribe. Soak up new knowledge and avoid discussing differences. Your goal is to watch and to understand what you could do with what you learn at a later point. This is part of being dormant in the learning and observing process. Your newly acquired understanding of the opposition will help you to argue, discuss, defend, attack, or represent your voice later.

Learn by being **honest**. That's a very underrated approach. Here's the thing: everyone lacks knowledge. And there definitely is no shame in saying, "I don't know." The shame would be the silence. Here's a great example: While in the corporate world, I attended many meetings. I was in management, however, I didn't have a college degree. I had been promoted through the ranks on street smarts and by learned knowledge (by doing). Many times in those meetings, someone would talk about something in a way that was not very clear to me. I thought it was because I lacked in book smarts, assuming everyone else in the room was more intelligent than me. Nonetheless, I wasn't afraid to interrupt the meeting (at a good point) to ask the meaning behind the thing that I didn't understand—only to find out that it hadn't been just me who failed to comprehend. So did most of the other participants. They had been too afraid to speak up. Imagine walking away with questions while having to perform follow-up items discussed in that meeting? If you do not understand, your work is going to be based on assumptions, and those assumptions could be off. Never be afraid to look like a fool for a minute versus making a complete and memorable idiot of yourself later. That silence will cost you much more and for much longer. If the presenter is unwilling to explain, then the shame is on them. It may not feel like it to you, but what does that say about the person refusing? They either don't get it themselves or they take pleasure in watching you struggle, or they may feel threatened by you. Whichever way, you must acknowledge that they have some issues to work on.

This also includes honesty and critical thinking. You will not learn correctly if you are not honest about yourself in any experience or by pretending that the reality of things aligns with your perception of what you want that reality to be. Whatever stage of learning you are in, admit that maybe it's not where you want to be, and then do the work to get there. Don't forget there's a foundation to everything we learn, so do not skip it just so that you can advance without having mastered the basics.

The same applies to mistakes. When you have made a mistake, commit to learning from it. Focus with honesty on why and how you have made that mistake, without blame. Could there have been a way to avoid it? Or multiple? Great. Would you have seen this approach without having made the mistake in the first place? Did you learn something else about yourself and your feelings? Did anyone contribute toward your feeling or failure? Acknowledge it all, learn from it, then let it go. Water under the bridge.

Whatever you learn, consider the purpose in all aspects of learning. What it is, what it means, what it represents, how it is done, where, when, why, for whom, in what capacity, for what result, etc. This may take some practice. To look at something and to appreciate it for more than its face value. Learn with purpose.

Learning is also about considering another angle. Sure, there may be a tried-and-true way, but why not step out of the expectations every now and then? Progress is never about sticking to the usual ways. Always consider what may be outside of the box.

The good news is that women are constantly analyzing something, not necessarily the right way, but we are great at spending tons of time thinking about things. We will use that to our advantage when it comes to all aspects of learning.

Of course, the more you know, the more you realize you don't know. In our quest to learn, the possibilities are endless. Because everything is connected, you can jump from one subject to another in the pursuit of mastery. I love it, and it doesn't intimidate me because I appreciate that I am able to pursue new things at my own pace. Think of learning as a puzzle where you get to connect the individual pieces as they happen to fit. You may come across pieces that don't work right away, but they will come together eventually.

The goal is not to start a hundred new or different things. That would be overwhelming. You'd give up on all of them eventually (sooner than later). Consider what is feasible for you, what excites you the most. Pick a few. Or pick just one. For starters, it could be one thing that you know is achievable, and that will set you up for success. Connect the dots slowly but with purpose.

Learning is about connecting (to everything, including yourself), and acknowledging that you can view the world with different eyes from different angles with a new appreciation of its beauty and value.

Learning about YOURSELF

In the pursuit of knowledge, you will undoubtedly learn a lot about yourself. Yet we learn a lot of things without paying much attention to ourselves, and hopefully this chapter will change your approach to learning and the revelations behind it. Learning should be about independent thinking and awareness. Critical thinking translates to evaluations based on evidence, facts, and observations to form rational judgments.

You cannot think critically (and do it well) if you are insecure in who you are. If you don't know who you are and what you represent (your values), then it's easy to become unsure of everything, leaving you vulnerable to be influenced or gaslit by others. Do not confuse thinking critically as being self-critical in subjective judgment. Yet the key is to learn about yourself in critical exploration first. I know it sounds messed up, but it is only when you know yourself that you will be honest and secure in your acceptance to where you can look at yourself and others, and the world, with the intended critical thought. If this doesn't make sense, no worries, because this book is part of your journey of understanding (yourself).

Simply remember that you must use anything you learn to help understand yourself. Below are a few great avenues in finding out who you are and what you stand for:

Pursue a hobby. I touched on this briefly earlier, but besides learning a new skill, a hobby can reveal a lot about yourself. Hobbies will teach you what you like or don't like, how well you deal with new things and situations, and what added strengths or weaknesses are yet to be discovered. Whatever hobby you pursue, it will bring out your insecurities. You must let them surface. Then you can move toward accepting and owning them, turning weaknesses into strengths.

For example, as a child, I always wanted to learn how to ride a horse, but it was an expensive hobby in Germany, where I grew up. My parents could not afford it. In my midtwenties, I started taking lessons at a barn. What I quickly realized was that horses had minds of their own, and they tended to ignore me. I could not get my horse to move forward into a good pace. Of course, it didn't help that my school horse had been around the block a few times, and he was not very motivated to lug another inexperienced, bouncy rider around. Most lessons resulted in me kicking the horse in an attempt to get him to go faster than the one mile per hour pace set by him. It goes without saying that my legs were typically worn out to the point of exhaustion, collapsing underneath me after dismounting, once the lesson was done.

My trainer kept encouraging me. He tried to talk me up. He had realized that I didn't have faith in myself, that I lacked confidence, and that I had never asked for anything assertively and expected results. Of course, I hadn't realized it fully at that point. I was aware that I lacked assertiveness, and at times, I got even more frustrated because I was aware that I lacked it, not knowing how to gain the needed confidence to be assertive. I should have celebrated the fact that I realized my shortcomings. Instead, I focused on only the negatives and got stuck, trying to cover up with false aids (by using a whip, which had more of an impact than me).

It took a while (meaning more life experiences and a willingness to work on myself) and a new mentor for me to be ready and willing to listen and observe and to look beyond what horseback riding truly meant when it came to my character. Sometimes, it takes time to be ready. A hobby can get you on your way.

Start writing. Could be a journal or diary. As the mood strikes, make entries about your day, emotions, ambitions, goals, and fears. Be honest and don't sugarcoat. While I realize that a tweaked version of events will sound less harsh and pathetic when you read it again later (or in the case you lose your journal and someone else gets to read it), try not to give in to that desire. It's the formulation of the words that will help you acknowledge a status, which will help you with your overall honesty (to yourself). The one person we most often lie to is ourselves. This will hurt you in the long run and could change how you see yourself. It will be stressful to maintain the lie when deep inside you know that you are only avoiding the inevitable. If you are worried about someone else reading your journal, then consider that you can always write down something that you can destroy immediately afterwards. The point is to get the words out. Alternatively, you could give the third-person point of view a try. You could create a short story, that, when read by someone else, can be understood as a work of fiction (and could be considered quite creative). For example, instead of, "I went crazy and took a baseball bat and pommeled a watermelon," you could write, "She could feel her anger rise from deep inside. Just thinking about the possibility of being fired for something she did not do made her furious. She saw the baseball bat in the corner behind the front door and smiled when she considered how the meeting would go if she brought it with her." While it's hiding the raw emotion, it is still a valid representation of that feeling of anger. You can really be creative, and in that sense, creative writing means letting your thoughts and words flow on paper unedited. Allow your thoughts to go where they want, write them down, and then let them go.

Several years ago, I took a sabbatical to write a memoir about the interactions with the men who have shaped my life. Initially, I had just wanted to vent over being a woman in the corporate man-world. A lot of my insecurities had stemmed from my father (of never measuring up), and they kept me from standing up for myself even after I had gotten to management. While I knew that my dad had had an impact on my current social behavior, I hadn't realized how much other people had contributed to that as well. In chronological order, I dedicated a chapter to either a good (Rick) or a bad (Dick) man from my life. Sometimes I had to think about whether a man had been a Rick or a Dick. That alone was a sad realization. Dissecting my life into chapters like that enabled me to have an objective view, on both the men and myself. I wasn't trying to judge the men or myself, the goal was to remain factual and honest, and I was forced to take a step back to evaluate. Things started to click for me.

I want to share a few (small) revelations. They may seem insignificant, but they were easy to notice and helped me to connect other dots. My dad forbade my sister and me from going to the bathroom at night. I know, sounds cruel, and my dad swears that it was never meant like that. He simply wanted a quiet house at night to let him sleep. The floorboards in our room upstairs creaked easily, and he could hear any movement below in his bedroom. He did not offer that explanation at that time, but it didn't matter. My sister and I followed our dad's commands to the tee. We were very young: I was around five, and my sister was seven years old. So, instead of physically going into our designated bathroom, my sister and I ended up peeing on our carpeted bedroom floor. We were quite successful for a while, covering it up with color blocks until the summer heat gave away our secret. The point is, even today, I always scope out where the bathroom is wherever I go. It used to stress me out NOT knowing where the bathroom was, no matter if I had the urge to go or not. Also, I often use the bathroom in the places I frequent because of fear of missing out. What if, all the sudden, I don't have access to a bathroom anymore? What if, on my way home, I have to urinate so badly, but there is no bathroom to be found? It's astounding (even to me) to realize how much this has impacted me. Probably because it would be such a humiliation if I had to pee myself in public if there wasn't a bathroom nearby. The point is that I had never acknowledged my anxiety over bathrooms until I wrote about my en suite carpet toilet in my childhood bedroom.

Here's another: I absolutely despise stupidly drunk people. A lot of us probably do. In my case, it brings back bad memories of my ex and some of the things he did when in a drunken stupor. Public humiliation (being screamed at), late night people-hunting sessions (guns loaded in the car alongside a case of Budweiser), and unwanted intercourse (giving in to appease the abuser) will do that to you. My defenses literally flare up when I get near really inebriated people. It's a fight or flight situation and something I have not fully mastered yet. But I'm aware of it, and I know why I feel that way.

Writing about the men in my life enabled me to dig up past experiences that have shaped my behavior, while I had absolutely no recollection of them having shaped my behavior in the first place, not to mention them still affecting me to this day. Let that sink in. There's power in the written word, but you may not see it until it has been written. And sometimes not until much later.

Listen. As touched on earlier, why not approach your family members for some feedback about you? I bet there were things you did as a child that still haunt you to this day. Your parents will share stories with love and laughter, sometimes tears, but they will affirm how great you are. Sure, some family members have nothing nice to say. Maybe use that opportunity to learn about them and not yourself. Outside of family, listening to people sounds easy, yet it turns out to be super hard for two reasons: First, we often only hear what we want to hear, and our perception and observation of a situation could be completely off. Second, because, well, people can be cruel in the way that they give feedback. Nonetheless, be open to feedback, criticism, advice, and teachings. Really take that opportunity to learn from others. Even when their perception of you is wrong. How others view you will be important in understanding how they will treat you and react to you in your interactions. Take it with a grain of salt when it comes to your perception of yourself. For example, at a performance review, don't think of yourself as a bad person because you have weaknesses or because you messed up. Feedback gives you the option to realize something of value or a perception or weakness to be disproved. Do not get defensive in the moment. Just listen and take it in. Simmer on it before reacting. This will be one of the hardest things you can do when receiving criticism. It's like that little reflex hammer that the doctor hits against your patellar ligament and your leg instantly comes up. Don't be that leg. Instead, acknowledge if the words spoken have hit a nerve. Why is that? Is it because it went against one of your core values, or is it because there is a kernel of truth? If your boss expects a response or a reaction, maybe just acknowledge that you heard the words and that you will need some time before offering a response.

Decide what you will do with that information. Here's an opportunity to grow if, in fact, there was some truth in the statement. Ignoring or shrugging it off will not benefit you. Also realize that not everything is to be taken personally. Not all bosses are out to get or demean you. Not everything you hear will be negative. We just tend to hear the bad things only. Pay attention to the positives. When a good boss gives criticism, they will also mention at least one of your strengths. It's called building you up before tearing you down, but it is meant to soften the blow to your ego. They don't want to hurt you, but it is their job to ensure that the business runs smoothly, and you happen to be part of that equation. Undoubtedly, no matter how well negative feedback is delivered, words can hurt. You must try to avoid lingering on any bad feelings and don't dwell on the negatives.

Listening with intent and an open mind can take communications to a new level. Imagine how much more productive your interactions will become if you and your opponent feel that concerns can be addressed without drama. (I have used the word "opponent" throughout this book to mean whoever you are facing visually in an interaction, not necessarily being of opposing views. Naturally, and as is often the case in interactions, it can represent the latter.)

Don't forget your mentors. They can teach without negativity, and they will give you great feedback about yourself and your performance. If you ask for their feedback, they will give it. And then there are your friends. More likely than not, you will find that your friends have a more upbeat view on you. Just the other day, I had a beautiful conversation with one of my best friends, in which he confessed blame for a recent breakup. His statement floored me. I didn't see him as insecure or at fault, having observed his unhealthy relationship over several years. He's such an empathetic person who gives more of himself in every relationship, and here he was believing that he had taken his partner for granted. A partner who went out of his way to control him through guilt and who had been overly protective of the relationship, so much so as to keep him away from friends while wooing him with his financial prowess, the overdoing of decorations, meals, and other intimate experiences. All while assuring him of their happiness because everything was picture perfect. Deflection can be evil. When you constantly look for blame within yourself, then it will be crucial for you to get some feedback from good-intentioned outside sources like your friends. Whatever you think is your biggest flaw, is probably a ruse created falsely by your mind, based on past experiences and behaviors as well as expectations by society and others who do not have your interest at heart. Maybe not all the time, but I want you to consider that you may have lied to yourself, resulting in a false perception.

Last but not least, listen to your body. If you can tune into your mental, physical, and emotional state, then you can address self-care quicker. Input equals output, yet we barely ever give any thought to cause and effect on our bodies with our daily routines (eating, exercising, etc.). I mentioned my fitness watch earlier in this chapter, and I do love it because it confirms some of my assumptions about how I think I'm doing physically. So many of us have undiagnosed health issues that pop up here and there, stay for a while, and then magically disappear. Doctors can't explain them, and tests may not show anything of value. But you know that there's something there. You can start a food journal or a health journal to see if you can find what triggers an event. The older I become, the more sensitive I am to sugar and alcohol. Every now and then I am plagued by joint and tendon pain. It pops up in different spots, sometimes lasting days, other times months. My fitness watch confirms that drinking alcohol puts a strain on my body, even while I sleep. What we put into our bodies has an impact on how we feel physically and emotionally. Start paying attention to what your body is telling you when you are feeling great, not so great, or when you feel bad. Learn what determines the level of health for you that you want to sustain.

Alongside physical signals, the same goes for your emotional ones. Become aware of your emotional state on good and bad days. Have there been any triggers for you? Consider activities or things you have been exposed to in the days prior or even moments before. I mentioned therapy in self-care already. However, talking with a therapist can also make you learn so much about yourself because you will be able to explore yourself in a safe, nonjudgmental environment, and there will be an expert who can help with acceptance and advice on how to overcome your obstacles. You may have something buried so deep inside of you that you aren't even aware of the hidden impact this something has on your everyday life and emotional state.

Even without a therapist, you will be able to learn about yourself if you are willing to be honest in accepting your emotional state as it happens. I find myself shrugging off my behavior or thoughts when I know that I'm not in a good place mentally (or when my actions are not so nice). It's then that I force myself to think about why I'm in such a funk. Typically, when I do that, it allows me to pivot my focus on something positive because I realize how petty I am being about something that has put me into this mood. The pivot happens as I admit that it is within my power to change my attitude, and that I was, up to that point, happy to reside in my misery. I'm talking about being in a funk, not in a mental crisis. Meditation, yoga, exercising, and religion are all things you can pursue to nourish your spiritually and overall well-being to prevent larger mood swings.

Undoubtedly, for prolonged issues and lingering emotions, I recommend professional help; but for the occasional rut, I'm sure you can affect change within if you are being honest with yourself.

Live life. Every day you add more life experiences and, with them, opportunities to learn more about yourself. Ageing works to your benefit. You know more today (about yourself) than you did yesterday. You would maybe even make different decisions today based on yesterday. The key is not to dwell on yesterday or the decisions you made then. Learn to move forward by learning from your past and the decisions made as there were reasons that drove you to make them. Understand your decisions so that you can realize your values.

And every coming day will help you make smarter decisions because you've learned something new or old about yourself while getting a clear image of what you value the most in life. Nothing more to be said, other than, live it.

Learning about THEM

When I refer to *them*, it means your opponent. Could be a true opponent (as in nemesis) or simply someone you're having a conversation with. This part can be fun because it makes you feel like you have control. And eventually you will (we get to that in the EMPOWER chapter).

You may be surprised how short this section is compared to the previous ones. There's a reason. Foremost, you must learn about yourself to truly understand where you came from, why you behave in certain ways, why you feel what you feel, what makes you tick, what interests you, etc. You need to become your own shrink. And once you know who you are, then you will also see others more clearly by default. For those doubters, I will throw some exercises at you later where we will examine them in more detail.

The good news, in general, is that the longer you **know someone,** the more you should know about them. If you don't, then I assume it's because you are a bad listener and observer, not because there has been an absence of participation on their part.

Tune your listening skills. This is not easy because most of us listen so that we can respond. And when I say respond, I mean in a way that draws attention back on us. We don't do this on purpose. We want to connect with the other person, but instead, we are bombarding them with news about ourselves to show similarities. You cannot learn about someone if you are not willing to listen to what they have to say. Listening is a strong tool when you do it for the right reasons. I'll spell it out: you need to listen so that you can collect information. The more information, the more accurate your assessment will be of them. You must learn as much as you can to help control your interactions and your emotions.

This also includes overhearing conversations. People love to talk about others. So don't ignore the people who know them. Gossip, events, small talk, and shared experiences are easy to come by if you talk to others—or are near them to overhear—in their or your circle. Keep it casual though; you don't want to draw too much attention to your research project. You're mining information, not trying to interrogate witnesses. Do not encourage and spread gossip. People will always be talking about someone (even you), and you get to decide what to do with that information. No need to instigate further gossip or trash talk, just listen. You will be able to learn how others view that person, and eventually, you will know whether you have allies or enemies to consider.

The gift of **observation** is one that I will address in more detail in the next chapter. Still, pay attention when you see them next. You'll encounter them everywhere: at work, school, sporting events, shopping centers, at home, in the gym—literally everywhere. Use each occasion to learn or confirm something. Pay attention to who they are with, how they act, what they wear, how they move, what they eat or drink, and where they are (environment).

Look at their social media. These days, seems like everyone uses social media to some extent (Facebook, Insta, Twitter, TikTok, LinkedIn, etc.). These platforms can tell you a lot about a person: What they like/dislike (religion, politics, worldview, food, hobbies, etc.), who their friends are, where they have worked, the content they share, who they write about, where and what they comment, who they follow. Guilty by association and self-promotion. Be aware, though, that some platforms will show who looked up a profile, so either avoid those platforms or ask a third party to call up that profile in your presence for anonymity.

And then, there's the rest of the internet, of course. It wouldn't be my go-to though. There's a high potential that you will reach wrong conclusions if you are only privy to a snippet of public information.

Experience them. You interact with them a lot, so let's use that. And yes, I get that you may not like dealing with them, but trust me, even in your current state, every interaction with them will teach you something about them. It could confirm a pattern or a certain response trigger, or reveal new data (opinion, worldview, background, etc.), which will serve as ammunition later. I bet it's not hard to engage them in conversations at all. Most difficult people have some type of enlarged ego, and you can use that to your advantage. They love talking about themselves. Even if it means that you must be fake nice, it will be worth it. And it matters not what they tell you; all of it is useful. And don't worry about being any good at steering the conversation yet. The intent is to expose yourself to them to get practice at noticing things (kind of like a spy does). It starts a pattern of training your brain and all your senses to become aware together. Another benefit of engaging them in small talk is that it will start the process of taking out the anxiety. Small talk is for exchanging pleasantries. It is not meant to dive into deeper subjects. Make the effort to be nice and to engage, and it will take the edge off in the long run. Your opponent will not see you as a threat or nuisance whenever you run into each other or have an interaction. They will be used to you and lower their defenses or aggressions. Face what you fear but start out facing what you fear in the best environment and under nonthreatening circumstances.

REFLECTIONS & EXERCISES

Here's where you must do the homework. But first, let me offer some honest reflection. When I read self-help books, I must admit, this is the part I typically skip. I hate the exercises because they slow me down from reading on. My goal is to finish the book, to get to the nitty-gritty. I'm not sure how I can convince you not to skip this part. This part is the nitty gritty. If you do plan on skipping, then here's some advice for consideration: At bare minimum, work through these exercises in your head. Just know that future exercises will build on previous ones.

Committing to written exercises will ensure better results because you will understand how you function as well as how others function once you see it in writing. As tedious as it may sound, there is a purpose, and you may not understand how the exercises fit together until later. Nonetheless, the emphasis is on seeing yourself factually and with honesty (without guilt, judgment, or shame).

I'm going to list a few starting points below that you can use to discover the real you. Think of these exercises as exorcisms. You are going to exorcise your demons if you can commit to learning about yourself by following this process.

Make a list of your weaknesses and your strengths.
Go ahead, start with your weaknesses. It will seem more intuitive because we tend to focus on our negatives over our positives. You may end up listing more weaknesses. That's okay. Keep in mind that your weaknesses can be worked on. You can list characteristics, and you can list skills that you perceive yourself to be bad at. That list alone can give ideas on where to focus your learning efforts. I wouldn't necessarily get hung up on your adjectives (e.g., weak, ignored, powerless). Focus on a skill set (e.g., great listener, good at math, excellent negotiator) because that in turn will help you with your confidence, which will help you to improve all your perceived character weaknesses.

If your list of strengths is super short, maybe ask a friend for some feedback (or a colleague, boss, relative). Nothing wrong with asking, "Hey, what do you like best about me?" or "What am I good at?" "What do you think is my biggest area for improvement?" Here it is important not to frame your question in a negative way (such as, "What am I bad at?"). When you can reframe questions to where they approach a reply geared toward criticism with a positive spin, then this will be a great tool in general for you. Help rewire your brain to view the negatives with more of an upbeat approach in the ask.

Do not do anything else with these lists yet, other than keep them safe and handy. As time passes, you can update your progress. It will be amazing to see how these lists change with each year that you are mastering L.O.V.E.! Strike through the weaknesses you nipped in the bud and keep adding those newly acquired strengths.

It is important to see it all in writing—as an acknowledgement of how and who you are now. And to use it to visualize and affirm your evolution.

Now for the fun part: Pick a person whose interactions you dread and determine what you know about them. Or pick a person who you are nervous about approaching (such as a boss about a raise).

Yup, simply go for that one person making your life miserable right now. What do you know about their background, school, job, spouse, children, education, clothes, habits, hobbies, routines, friends, bosses, subordinates, interests, relationships, health, finances, church, religion, beliefs, etc.

Focus on writing down short notable facts (no characterizations or emotions). Don't worry if at first you don't come up with many points. We will add more later.

Let me give you an example:

The Napoleon

Owner of company, blond, middle-aged German with an overall look of **European young urban professional** (designer jeans, Ed Hardy shirts, bold eyewear, ecological footwear, big jewelry). **Short** in size, **normal build. Two McMansions** on the lake in the States, a **house in Germany, German-engineered sportscar, several Harleys,** lover of

Apple products, **well traveled**, **likes to cook**, **owns a fancy coffee machine (barista type)** and mostly **German appliances**. German **wife** and **two children (daughter eldest, then son)**. **Deceased father** who founded the company. **Several sisters** in Germany. Company **locations in Germany, U.S., and China**. **Not at office** a lot when in country. Sufficient **English skills**, attempting to **learn Chinese**. **Hobbies: spending money**. **No visual health issues**. **Likes to shake hands**.

Keep it as simple as possible (you will know what it means, so no need to expand or explain). The bolded items above really highlighted to me what was notable about Napoleon. You can do the same with your character(s).

That's it for this chapter. Good job sticking with the exercises. And even though this chapter was very long, all you really have to remember is that every moment lived, is an opportunity to learn.

Let's move on to the next step in the L.O.V.E. process, which is observation. Are you ready to see your world in a new light?

CHAPTER 2: OBSERVE

Observation is an instinctive and spontaneous component of the learning process.

For starters, I want to define the two basic types of observers that apply to you for this book's purpose, but it really does not matter which one you are.

The Participant Observer

As the name states, this is when you participate in whatever it is that you are observing, whether it is in a group, at an event, in an interaction, in a game, etc. Your other participants will, of course, notice you and your participation. This includes your encounters with your opponent no matter how active or inactive you present yourself while in them.

Non-Participant Observer

Again, no huge revelation here. When you observe without participating, then you are a non-participant observer. You could be in a group, at an event, online, etc. All you do is observe without any type of action. You have no intention to participate. As a non-participant observer, you may or may not be visible to others, and others may or may not notice your presence. It's when you (excuse the term) spy on your opponent that you are a non-participant observer with a purpose.

What comes to mind when you think of observation? Seeing, hearing, smelling, tasting, feeling? It is true that all our senses are involved when we observe; maybe not all at once, but nonetheless, our senses are ready to observe when engaged. And our senses are engaged when we observe. You can't do one without the other. However, during interactions, there is so much data thrown our way, it is impossible to notice everything. Yet the data exists.

In a more boring context, think of observation as research. Unfortunately, we often let that research squander because it seems too overwhelming to acknowledge or process. Honing our brains to help process this flow of data so that we become aware of it will take time and practice; however, the awesome news is that your brain is, and has been, at the ready (when you are ready). Everything you experience (observe) is received and acknowledged by that beautiful, complex organ, and it saves this data. You should be able to access this information when you go looking for it later. Nothing is ever lost completely.

The act of observing can be fun and enlightening. You literally do this every day. You just need more awareness to use observation as an enabler. And while awareness is key, observation should be done with the least amount of opinion possible. Here, once again, honesty must prevail. So, as you observe with intent, you must ask yourself if you are letting other factors influence your observations. Other factors could be past experiences, mainstream media or opinions, expectations, hearsay, gossip, etc.

And while you can use your experiences to validate observations, you must be honest enough to admit that your findings can change at any time, pending new data/observations.

Herein lies the challenge. We tend to observe with prejudice and judgment, and then form more opinions, which in turn, makes us even more opinionated when observing next.

Let me give you an example to put this into context:

People used to ask me, "Do you believe men can change?"

Yes, that's a heavy and loaded question.

I used to be quick to answer, "Not really."

The answer was more of an instant knee-jerk reaction than truthful. See, my reply was rooted in a false approach. Because the larger picture on women's rights has not changed dramatically in recent decades, I did not think men could fundamentally change because men weren't fundamentally willing to change. My answer was also based on my ex-husband, the alcoholic, who had attempted to quit drinking on more occasions than I have fingers and toes to count. He failed to become sober, and he was complacent with his condition and treatment of me. I had been shaped by my bad experiences which, when asked the question, pushed themselves to the top of my thoughts, demanding vocal revenge by way of generalization.

This perception changed when I wrote a book about my life—and the general oppression by the men in it—which I presented to a local women's group where that same question was posed by a woman in a difficult relationship. My instinct was to give the same answer as before. But I couldn't. Something stopped me. I had made an observation that something felt different. The feeling was one of dishonesty. The "no" sat on my tongue, but all the flavors were wrong. Here I was, a woman's advocate, about to say that men typically don't change based on what fact? Here I was, a woman's advocate, who once had been a timid, insecure, and powerless adolescent. As I looked around the room, I saw change screaming at me. I saw women who had cut their hair, lost weight, got divorced, quit jobs, started companies, etc. Everyone changes all the time. For better or worse, but we'd be fools to think we don't.

The true and honest answer is that men can change. All humans have that capacity if they are willing to make an honest effort.

What do you think triggered my hesitation this time (a.k.a. observation)? I had been asked that question before. Well, I was usually asked that question in a more private setting. Typically, by women in abusive relationships, who I felt should move on. Those women hoped for that change, needed to hear me say it to justify staying with their abusers since there would still be hope that they could change them into something better. Unfortunately, most abusers do not change unless they experience a major breakdown. A breakdown that could cost women the ultimate price. My instinctual answer was to protect them. I could not give them false hope to stay in a toxic relationship.

Something was different in the circumstance and environment that impacted me to change my answer this time: I was giving my speech in a larger setting to strong female business owners. I wanted to establish myself as a reputable and serious speaker and women's advocate. I realized that I could not generalize all men into evil beings in this environment and walk away knowing that I had spoken the truth or accomplished my goal. It would have been a disservice to women and men alike.

When you look at the facts, you cannot deny them and maintain your integrity. Words matter, all the time. My audience would have never taken me seriously if I had said that men don't change. Because what truly is the purpose for anyone advocating for something? Exactly. Advocates advocate for CHANGE, and here I was advocating for women. Fundamentally, an advocate must believe that change is possible or there would be no reason to fight for the betterment of anything.

How about those abused women? I still believe that leaving is the right answer when it comes to those relationships that have a long history of oppressive abuse. But now when I say, "Yes, men can change," I make sure to include that success is unlikely if the abuse has been ongoing, and the abuser is unwilling to talk, admit, accept, and then make moves to change accordingly. There can never be deflection. Only honesty. It's okay to try to impact change, but some people are not ready or willing. Do not continue to waste your efforts on haters. They are not worth it.

The people we can change for sure? Ourselves!

I chose the above example because you probably have never considered observation from that perspective where it forces an internal pause. Think about it though. If you say something aloud (or think it before deciding to speak it) and it feels wrong, then you have observed with awareness. And sometimes, when you say things without conviction and strength in your tone, that's another example of a hidden truth acknowledged (observed). There's something inside you that makes you hesitant, scratches your conscience, and feels insincere. It's the voice of your values that speaks to you internally. Maybe that's what we call the benefit of the doubt. When it occurs, then we should stop and revisit our thoughts. And then take another look with honesty at our observation and data collected that should form our (revised) responses and opinions.

In a perfect scenario, our brains would collect data without an abundance of influencing factors (such as opinions and experiences). Then my initial answer to "Can men change?" would have been more considerate and truthful from the get-go. Unfortunately, as adults, we have gone through a lot, and that adds to our distortion of our views. (However, I do not want to disvalue the fact that our experiences can, in fact, validate our observations.)

It seems that the only opportunity for unbiased observation happens when we are babies. Okay, so that ship has sailed for all of us, but hopefully, you get the point I'm trying to make. Observing is the only way babies learn at first, and babies are quick to adapt based on their observations. This is so intuitive. Think about it (they don't). Babies are not born with complex thought processes or malicious intent to manipulate. They live in the moment. When they are hungry, they will let you know because they will cry. When their diapers get nasty, they will cry (and so will you). They don't like something, they will cry. Crying is their tool to get your attention in their moment of need. And it works like a charm.

Being in the moment is important in your journey to empowerment. Unfortunately, most grown-ups do not live in the moment. We create false perceptions. **We are stuck in the past, worried about the future, and so we get lost in the present.**

My goal is to make you be in the moment with awareness and honesty by simply focusing on how you observe. It will take a real effort to silence the busyness (noise) in your head in the beginning. We are so preoccupied with our previous interactions, emotions, and fears that we forget to live this moment, and just like that, this moment lost has been added to all the other wasted moments before. You cannot change the past by not living the moment and by worrying about the future.

When you try to observe something, you must be seeing that something in the moment without judgment. There's no time to worry or think about yourself, no need to conjure up past experiences or feelings. You cannot bring other people's perceptions, beliefs, or opinions into it either. Look at the moment, and maybe for the first time, see it for what it is, not what you assume it to be.

Observational Mirrors

How about **planting yourself in front of an actual mirror** for some one-on-one time? Just you and your awesome visage face to face. What do you see? Go ahead, do it. What's your best feature? And why? What's your least favorite? By the way, I didn't say worst feature for a reason. There are none, and you need to accept that. Make peace with your face. Your friends love it; they recognize you by it, and besides, they see your beauty from the inside.

Case in point: When someone asks me if one of my friends is pretty or handsome, I always respond in accordance with what they hold inside. How I value them, what they give me, and if they are trying to do good in the world. I don't have any ugly friends. The same applies to your friends. They determine your beauty by your actions and values, and if they are your true friends, then I bet they don't think of you as ugly either.

Back in the day, I used to hate my smile. In school, kids made fun of my big teeth and my large mouth. It got so bad that I would place my hand over my mouth when I spoke. Nonetheless, my big smile is my best feature and uniquely mine. "That's so Petra," my friends will say. Even strangers have commented on my smile. When I think a photo of me is dreadful, one of my friends will surely say how much they love it. They always see something positive because they know my value to them, even if they don't realize having done so. Always agree when someone compliments you. You must realize that there is nothing ugly about you. If someone does not see your beauty, then they don't deserve to be around you.

Speaking of beauty, let's return to the mirror exercise. Choose an adjective (e.g., sad), and make a face that goes with the word. Keep going: mad, happy, delirious, surprised, sympathetic, proud, exasperated. Do you believe your face? Don't be afraid to be overdramatic. Pay attention. A bit of your performance translates into your actual facial expressions in real life situations. Your face involuntarily responds to everything (those little twitches or movements are called microexpressions), and it is impossible to hide them. I have a ton of microexpressions happening in my face, and they are very noticeable. A smirk, a quick blink, a twitch in my nose, a tight dimple, etc. My face will always tell you how I feel about what you're saying or doing.

The goal with this little exercise is to become comfortable and to take comfort in the mirror. The person you see in the mirror is your past and present. I hope you see your potential. If you don't see it yet, don't worry, because a bit farther down this L.O.V.E. road, you will undoubtedly.

I also want to mention body language as it is a mirror to our feelings. Crossed arms may be a sign of internal defenses kicking in or an internal need for protection. People who like each other or who are of the same mindset often adjust their bodies in the same position; sometimes this is true for people who are seen as leaders. I get a kick out of my friends because when we hang out together, we tend to mirror our gestures, body positions, and even language in just a matter of minutes. Sometimes, I change my arm position intentionally and see how long it takes for my friends to mirror me. It's a fun game you can play in your mind. See who changes first, and maybe you can notice whose body language you are copying yourself. It happens so naturally; it will amaze you. How about that impact? It's like a secret power as it can tell you how people feel about each other.

I encourage you to pay attention in your next meeting how people are sitting. Are they starting to mirror each other? Who sits where? Next to whom? Are people facing each other or facing away from each other? Who interrupts, leans in, speaks over others? Who is respectful of input or questions? Anybody with involuntary microexpressions, such as a tiny frown, a nose ruffle, a smidgeon of an eyebrow raise?

Our faces and bodies say a lot about our opponents. The good news is, so do theirs, and since they are not aware of theirs, we can take advantage of that (eventually).

Another mirror observation opportunity is (video) **self-recording**. Say what? Glad you asked. Could be doing your favorite hobby, reading a book aloud for a few minutes, or pretending to be interviewed on camera. It may sound a bit stupid or silly, but it's not. The reason is that you cannot hide in front of a camera. I'm willing to bet that most of us don't like to see ourselves in recordings because we fear that it will show our insecurities and weaknesses or that we would look ridiculously untalented. Nonetheless, it is the most objective representation of an action or a behavior. Recording yourself will also show you how others see you. Think about how you observe someone or something. Try to see yourself as another person; remove yourself from you, including any feelings. Simply watch without prejudice and see the action.

When it comes to recording an activity (such as a hobby or sport), you may need to volunteer a friend to help take that precious footage. Have them decide when to record. It should be honest footage, not staged, if you want to see something of new value. Sometimes, the best footage shows us at our worst. When you watch it back (by yourself), ignore any emotions that come up and really see the action for what it is. Does your body language say anything at any given time? As an outside viewer, how did you handle yourself in that recording? And then you can also be honest with your feelings in that moment. Just like that, you have connected your outward image to an inside emotion.

I would advise that you rewatch any such recording after a few days have passed. You will find that you were often unjustly harsh in your first assessment of yourself. Be more forgiving the next time you watch. See the positives. They are there if you are willing to acknowledge that you do not suck at everything. You don't.

Years ago, I was invited to give a twenty-minute speech at a women's organization. It was my first talk in my role as a women's advocate, and it was quite daunting. I'm a writer, not a speaker, so I was anxious. Nonetheless, I came up with a speech outline on paper, and then I recorded myself giving this speech in my living room, over and over. Watching those clips gave me several observations. I articulated a lot with my arms and hands, and my mouth made a lot of weird movements (microexpressions)—but only if I got stuck or didn't like how something came out of it (typically, differently than I had planned). I loved that I didn't look too rigid; I got better with more practice, and I accepted that I couldn't master this new challenge on the first try because it takes practice. It always does.

Seeing myself, as an outside observer, gave me a better image of how others perceive me and how I present myself to them when out of my comfort zone.

Give it a try. Maybe you have posted some videos on social media already? That's great. If you rewatch them now, what can you observe that you didn't notice the first time? Try out slow motion. Some expressions really become obvious that you were not able to notice earlier.

The next point goes hand in hand with visual recording because, well, most videos will also have sound. So **listen up**. For example, I had always thought that my voice sounded horrible. Watching and hearing myself give my speech changed that perception. Turns out, I quite like my voice; it sounded pleasant and non-offensive. At the same time, my German accent wasn't as slight as I had imagined it to be, and it felt like a huge betrayal. I thought my accent was a weakness because my pronunciation wasn't perfect, which made me more vulnerable to criticism and less credible. Being an immigrant (foreigner) in America has its own set of challenges, and there are many ways to observe prejudices about intelligence when a speaker is non-native. Let me explain. As a German American, when I speak, some people give me that exasperated look. If you're not familiar with the look, it's the "move your head forward and tilt it sideways, squint your eyes, and read my lips" look. Often, I am asked (in a loud voice) to repeat myself because it must have sounded like an alien or idiot was speaking. I know I'm not that hard to understand, but I have learned that this behavior can say a lot about a certain type of person (they've been sheltered; they don't know any other languages or cultures; they've never left the U.S.; they lack education—it's actually their weakness, not mine). My German accent is, in fact, a unique feature, an identifier of my awesomeness, and I have started to embrace it.

Here's another example of what audio has taught me about myself: I had the glamorous idea that I should do a podcast. But, as I have described earlier, I'm a writer, not a speaker by nature, and I have a hard time speaking freely for long periods. Freely is to be understood as unrehearsed, free flowing, continuously, and without detailed notes. I recorded a tiny spiel about people littering. Took me an hour to record five minutes. Yes, I could speak about what ailed me, but all in all, that took less than one minute. I'm a get-to-the-point speaker, I hate embellishing a story with overt distractions, and I feel fake filling dead silence with colorful nonsense. Other observations: I wasn't funny or passionate in my delivery. My enunciation sucked. I sounded fake to my own ears. Not at all like I had envisioned it in my head. However, it was just another item to add to my improvement list. What a great tool to understand why my comfort lies in writing. Natural speaking—or free speaking—is something that I need to cultivate and practice. I'd probably known this for a while, but I had chosen to bury this in the back corner of my brain. I had faked myself into thinking that I would be a great podcaster from the get-go. Being an advocate should make it easy to speak freely, but there's a difference between rambling on incoherently versus cohesively educating an audience. Words need to be funneled strategically.

You could record yourself reading a section from a book, talking about something you are passionate about, ranting like I tried, etc. When listening to your audio, what can you observe? Are there a lot of ahem, um, eh, or uh sounds? Did you stay on point? Was your grammar correct? Did it flow? How was your pronunciation? Did you sound anything like you had imagined?

How about **using animals** as observational mirrors? Animals, all living in the moment, can teach us about who we are in any moment. Like babies, animals are not born with complex thought processes or malicious intent to manipulate. They are the ultimate tools in becoming self-aware. I was very fortunate that my hobby involved horses, which allowed me to observe a lot about myself (and them).

After decades of lessons and thinking that I had mastered the basics, I half-leased an awesome little gelding at a horse farm. At that barn, I continued taking occasional lessons, and that's when things started clicking for me. The trainer there was into natural horsemanship. In short, this means that instead of trying to force a horse into submission, the approach is one of partnership. To be one with the horse. Side note: I want to recognize that I did miss a big opportunity to learn about myself when I first started horseback riding. My brain wasn't in tune with my awareness, I lacked individual thought, and I was stuck thinking that there was only one way to be taught. I was simply going through the motions. I rode horses, but I felt clueless and stalled in my training. Going through the motions is not the same as progressing to the next level. Let's acknowledge that sometimes we are not ready to learn more than what we are able to handle mentally and physically at that point in time. It's not easy to become unstuck in life. Think of your car's transmission being in PARK. The car just sits there. It is ready to be driven, but something must happen first before shifting into NEUTRAL, and then DRIVE.

I made it to the neutral stage by watching and taking lessons from this new trainer. She opened my eyes to the fact that I had never considered the me in the equation nor a partnership of equals. Lessons always started out with groundwork (this is where you work the horse on the ground before getting on) and served as an evaluation phase. I had done groundwork before. What was different though was that this trainer observed the horse, and she explained how the horse was observing her. This evaluation phase was the foundation for determining how the actual ride would go, all dependent on the horse's mind, the rider's awareness, the environment, and the rider's emotional state. This was news to me.

My trainer was right. Horses are instant and honest in their evaluation of humans, and their reactions give the answers of their observations.

Some examples: If you walk up to a horse with a negative attitude and/or with a speed or energy too angry or too fast, the horse will receive you with less joy and with nervous anticipation. The same applies if you are insecure or unsure of yourself, the horse, or the situation. Chances are the horse will walk or run away from you once you get close. This used to happen to me a lot in the past. The horse trusts its instinct and its perception of the way things are in that moment. If your energy is all wrong (you are upset, angry, not settled, not calm, not focused, insecure, not in the moment), then the vibes you are giving off to the horse will make it not want to be near you. If you are going into a ride with the wrong intention, the horse will know the purity of your heart and thoughts. It has no agenda, but it will know yours instantly. You must be the calm, confident, and protective leader they love to follow.

I had always approached riding as an activity that I did and had never valued the horse as a reactive being to my behavior or emotions. The horse was a tool—a means to an end. What a narrow mindset. Yet most of us do not appreciate the value something can give us.

With my mind and eyes open, I started to observe the big signals. What was the horse doing, and what signals was it giving? Where were its ears pointing? Toward me or away from me? Where was the horse's body in relation to mine? There were a lot of visuals that I could detect because they were obvious and large (now that I had adjusted my awareness level). Others, my trainer had to teach me. It wasn't long before I started observing myself through the horse's eyes. Were my shoulders open to it, or was I scrunched up in my heart/chest? Was there tension in my shoulders, arms, hands? Did I hold my breath while working/handling the horse? Was I happy and focused? Or had I come to the barn with all my emotional baggage?

By simply changing the focus to a partnership, my trainer had helped me put that lever into NEUTRAL. Think of neutral as being an objective view. I started taking the emotion out while trying to see my environment in its entirety with me in it. For me, it was the first time that I understood the concept of having an impact on something without purpose; I had let things happen without awareness. It motivated me immensely that with intent, I could change my impact. Impact happens with or without your awareness. Would I mind putting in some work to get to DRIVE? Not at all. This realization and attitude change helped me move out of PARK into NEUTRAL.

Paying attention to myself, and then to the horse's reaction to me, showed that I had a lot of doubt. I lacked confidence, and the horse would notice that and act accordingly. When a horse doubts you as its leader, it will do two things: (1) ignore you, and (2) take over and assume leadership to ensure its survival.

I had run into this issue from day one in my quest to ride horses. I could not hide my insecurities or emotions from them. Nobody can. Animals have you figured out in a nanosecond. They are experts at noticing everything, and the tiniest of details can have an impact. I learned that if I can acknowledge how an animal/horse reacts to me, then there is the potential to change that.

For now, it is more important that you realize that you can learn a lot about yourself if you change your viewpoint or your approach. A new hobby will almost always make you see yourself differently than before. You must be aware of your observations (and those of others in their teaching).

A note of encouragement: Trying to observe yourself through your own eyes and other lenses can seem impossible at first. Sometimes we don't want to see; other times the cues may be too small to notice. Do not let the immensity of the task discourage you from trying. There is always a starting point, and that could be different for each of us. The point is that you must start somewhere, and why not start with one thing large and obvious? Think about it. In the pursuit of a hobby, what has been your biggest hurdle? Whatever it is, focus on one thing you can try differently. Set the expectation small. Success is measured in the tiniest of accomplishments. Be patient with your observation skills. Time is on your side as you hone that talent.

Using the fleeing horse as an example, one way to overcome this challenge could be by altering your emotional and mental state prior to heading into the pasture. Breathing exercises, meditation, stretching, inner reflections, waiting ten minutes to focus—before you try to get your horse—can help settle your inner self. This will change your aura and the way the horse perceives you. However, you must also have the confidence in yourself to be the leader the horse wants you to be. This approach would never be my first choice—seeing that achieving a centered, calm self takes a lot of awareness, which most people do not possess naturally—but it should be the ultimate goal.

The easier approaches are: to either have someone put the horse in its stall before getting there (if the horse tends to run away in the pasture) or walk up to the horse with its favorite treat in hand. It's not cheating when you use an approach that you feel will have a high success rate as a temporary solution while you are trying to get to your permanent fix. However, do not get stuck on your temporary solution.

The point is, if something isn't working the way you have always done it, then think of another method. There are always multiple solutions you can try. You can also find another mentor/teacher if you find yourself unsuccessful.

Persistence is key. And not getting stuck on one approach if it is not working.

Don't have a horse? No problem. Any animal will do. Dogs and cats are great teachers, but I must say that dogs are more willing and obvious. If your dogs don't listen in general, then they don't accept you as their pack leader. This probably means that you are not assertive in the moment, and your indecision or absence of clarity are observed by them. Dogs (and horses) want pack leaders because it is very stressful for them to make their own decisions. They would rather you make decisions for them. Horses, especially, have survived only because they ran away from everything. For animals, it is about trust in you as a leader to make the right decision in the moment. But decisions have to be made in a clear, assertive, and calm way. That doesn't come naturally to most humans.

Watch your dogs, cats, or other critters at any given time and observe how they act and interact. Seriously, consciously observe their actions and reactions. How do they act when you are stressed or happy? Do they flinch when you reach out to pet them? What happens when you have a visitor come to your house? Is your dog charging to the door every time, ready to tackle whoever comes inside while barking uncontrollably? And where are you when this happens? How do you react? What's its favorite toy, treat, game, walk? Who's its favorite person? Is there someone your animal dislikes? Are there any cues to social behaviors when your animal is in its pack (you included)? Who is more dominant?

Any pet will work if you pay attention to its behavior and yours, and the corresponding reactions. You may not understand the reasoning behind every (re)action, but eventually, you will be able to draw conclusions that can be confirmed through repetition or by changing your own behavior to see if it impacts change. Alternatively, you can read books about pet behavior and training or watch series on animal trainers who treat their subjects with compassion and understanding. Undoubtedly, you will observe something of value.

Observational Lenses

Observational lenses allow you to watch others and yourself. Obviously, observational lenses include the above mirror observations. When reviewing (observing yourself in) any of the exercises mentioned in the previous section as a non-participant observer, the goal is to watch and listen factually without prejudice while staying emotionally neutral. Make objectivity your observational lens in any observation.

Hearing the word "observation," we tend to think of watching others more than ourselves. People watching is a favorite pastime for me. I'm constantly looking for interesting characters or conversations to reuse in my books. But I also pay close attention to people in general because of the wealth of information that comes along with it.

Do not miss out on observing those around you that you must deal with consistently. At work, this will be a wonderful tool. Pick a boss or coworker whom you despise or fear, and watch them. How do they walk? Does that say anything about them? Do they greet or acknowledge others as they pass? Shake hands? Make eye contact? How do they leave the break room when they are done? Do they ever clean up? Make coffee? Offer to help? You will see a lot. This also works for your heroes, mentors, and role models. What makes you admire them? What is the environment and/or circumstance you are observing them in? Can you tell when they are comfortable/uncomfortable or when they have an impact on others? Watch with purpose and without instant judgment or confusing noise. You can use that opportunity to add your observations to the list (what do you know about them) that you started in the previous chapter.

These non-participant observations can also be done at home. Watch the news, game shows, infomercials, etc. If you pay attention, you will be able to get an idea of what people are feeling in the way they express themselves verbally and visually through body language and microexpressions. Watch with purpose.

Of course, others may be observing you. Unintentionally or intentionally, with or without purpose, with admiration or disrespect. Observation happens all the time whether you notice it or not.

Observation of Appearances

I'm not saying to judge based on appearances. But there's so much to be learned when looking at someone. Could there be clues here on how that person wants to be viewed or perceived? Take me, for example. My hair is super short; sometimes I sport a fauxhawk; I got tattoos; I dress casually; I wear no make-up, flaunt no perfume, and I don't accessorize. I'm a walking oxymoron, fighting for women's rights but trying to look as manly as I can. Or am I? There's truth in that statement. But there's also more: I'm lazy and I love to sleep in. I don't have to mess with my hair, and once out of the bathtub (I don't shower), it takes me less than three minutes to style. I also don't like hiding behind hair, and I'm quite happy with my face and my awesome smile. In short, my hair is not a distraction. I wear jeans and T-shirts because I like to be comfortable. Working from home, I'm known to answer my door in a onesie. I despise the expectation of how people in corporate America want you to look. I'm a rebel. And btw, yes, that fauxhawk is supposed to call attention to me in a statement of "I am not compliant with your standards" (= I'm different). Dressing up now and then can be fun, but I'm not going to waste my money on appearances for the sake of others. It's just not me. I own it.

At the same time, I don't knock dressing nicely. Clothes make us; I do not deny it. And some clothes can make you feel powerful, beautiful, sexy. They can have purpose. I have some nice clothes (somewhere). It's also a question of money. If I were rich, I'd have some fancier, still comfortable clothes that would enhance my appearance. Yes, we are what we wear (and yet we aren't).

If your job requires a certain dress code, then your wardrobe needs to adapt, which may not be to your liking. You can still be honest about your feelings when looking at yourself in the mirror. Our environment plays a huge role in our decision-making process, and you should be aware of that.

I want to offer an interesting thought. Sometimes I wonder why I have more male supporters than female. For one, based on my experience, it is hard to motivate women into action for their own causes. More on that later. Maybe men are more apt to support me because my outward look is nonthreatening to them, which makes them (and me) more approachable, and, I bet, relatable. A lot of men are intimidated by an overly costumed and made-up woman, and they will not know how to approach her or how to interact. There's nothing in common at first glance, and there will be little effort made in trying to understand her; they may even be hostile or condescending out of fear and insecurities. As weird as this may sound, consider if appearances could have an impact on how men see us as either foes or allies. Case in point: My visual appearance, my assertiveness, and my strong presence at past jobsites have resulted in many men answering to me with, "Yes, sir." What does that tell you about women (me)? Seems that men instinctively respond to what is perceived to be male behavior with a male affirmation because they are too perplexed that this behavior came from a strong woman (who looks like a man). Strong female leadership behavior is neither expected nor wanted as it shatters men's perceptions of weak and emotional women. There is no such thing as male traits when it comes to leadership. Just like there are no female traits when it comes to emotions. Those "traits" are simply taught behaviors and beliefs. They are not owned by either gender, and we need to stop others when they genderalize.

So . . . look at your wardrobe, your accessories, your car, your coffee brand, your social activities. What do these items say about you? You have an image, and so does everyone else.

Just for fun, I'm going to list general observations of a former peer, a VP of Sales: Male, late twenties, introvert, about 5'5", stocky build but not overweight, wearer of casual pants with polo shirts, a college ring, a wedding band designed to match the college ring, driver of a new Mercedes SUV, husband to taller wife (with a vision and pants), drinker of energy drinks, avoider of people, hider behind desks, pleaser to his boss, non-delegator of work.

Do you think that you could draw some conclusions based on this very short description? Give it a thought before reading on.

Here we go: This boss stayed in his office all day, hiding behind his desk because he feared confrontation, conflict, and human interaction. When he left his office, he would walk quickly and silently to his chosen destination, eyes to the ground because he didn't want to be noticed. Or if he was noticed, he could avoid engaging in a conversation by keeping his eyes glued to the ground, blocking out his environment. He spoke softly and intelligently. He was great at strategizing and spreadsheets. He had been a salesperson before being promoted to the company's VP after the general manager had left. He was quick to say "yes" to everything his superiors wanted (because he feared confrontation), no matter how much time and effort it required of him. He would rather work evenings and weekends than to delegate any of the work to others because he knew he could do it quicker and better (and he hated to ask for help). He did not lie, but he did not speak the truth at times to avoid lying. Sometimes, he simply didn't say anything at all. He loved his college. He loved his wife. He had a good heart because he saw the good in people.

Lots of information there. None of my observations are mean or untrue. They are all based on my experiences over a period of time, and he has proven my assumptions to be factual. None of this means that he is, or was, a bad person. He had the best intentions. Despite his efforts, he was an ineffective leader because he lacked in a lot of areas, such as trust, confidence, support, and experience. **Bad bosses do not necessarily translate into bad people.** You must make that distinction, and you must be fair in your assessment. When it comes to appearances, you can attempt to judge a book by its cover, but keep an open mind that the content may not be what the cover advertises. And sometimes it is.

Keep learning and observing.

Observation of Action (Them & You)

Once you practice the art of observation on animals and yourself, then looking at other people's appearances and interactions can become second nature. To get to that stage, a conscious effort and connection must be initiated first. For example, try to link how someone shows up to work every day in appearance to how they show up in the sense of action and energy. How do they drive, park, enter a room/building, greet others, walk, speak, interact, etc.? Up until now you have seen these things, but you really haven't paid any attention. You can learn so much by simply tuning in to your environment.

Connecting an appearance to action—or knowledge to action—is a tool in your brain that you have underutilized to date. Our brains store all that our eyes see. The data is there. Accessing it has been the problem. As mentioned previously, while you saw, you were blind. Blind to all the clues happening right in front of you. It is why we must train our consciousness to utilize observations with a purpose.

It takes effort to tap into your consciousness. Having shifted into NEUTRAL meant for me that, at work, I paid more attention to how people reacted to me. How did they sit behind the desk when I approached? Did their facial expression change? Did they cross their arms? Where were they seated during my interactions? Behind the desk? Sitting up higher on the edge of the desk? Looking down on me? Over my shoulder? How did they say things? In what tone, loudness, clarity? Just like the horse had been a mirror, I saw that people were no different. If I walked out of a meeting feeling bad, then I started thinking about how I had gone in, how my facial and body expressions must have looked, and how I had said what I had said, e.g., tone, loudness, clarity. With each replay of an event, I would see things clearer and more objectively. Instead of taunting myself—if one of my approaches had been less than open (resulting in a bad reaction)—I acknowledged it and envisioned how I would do it differently next time. I practiced interactions. I played out different answers and movements in my head and tried to anticipate my opponent's answers or counterpoints. I mentally prepared myself for the next meeting.

This anticipation of various possible situations gave me more confidence and control going into subsequent encounters. Because I had thought through the scenarios, I knew what to expect next, and it helped me adapt my attitude and my responses in that moment.

As women, we often get caught up in our weaknesses. The focus tends to be on the bad things that happen in life. We get stuck in the repetitive cycle of self-doubt by reliving bad memories or past mistakes and by self-analyzing and questioning all our decisions. While that is an important step in learning about yourself, somehow, women get detoured ninety-nine percent of the time. Instead of believing that we can move forward and avoid similar outcomes next time, we believe that the results will be the same or worse. Women are psyching themselves out of their own solutions. This cycle needs to be broken, and the way to achieve that is by taking out the emotions when reliving the moment.

Observation of Emotions (Triggers)

In the business world, emotions are frowned upon. Women have the reputation of being emotionally unstable. Yet we know this to be untrue, and it can be clearly observed in everyday life where men's emotions get the better of them all the time.

Emotions are awesome. There's nothing wrong with them. Everyone experiences them. Acknowledge that. They can have a good or bad influence over our decisions, and they definitely have an impact on how we react to others. Emotions are triggers. What's a trigger? A trigger triggers you to react in a certain, predestined, and consistent way. Most of the time, we feel out of control when they happen. Triggers apply to good and bad feelings. They are powerful when it comes to your interactions and are always coupled with emotions.

In your observations of them, watch out for emotional expressions, such as phrases or gestures, that precede an action. You will know you hit a trigger because something will be very obvious in a behavior. Could be a one-eighty, meaning, going from a nice conversation to a conflict in an instant. There had to be something to cause such a shift. Someone blushing, breathing heavily, encroaching your space—those are all reactions to something that preceded the action. Cause and effect. You must view the interaction differently to realize that everyone has an impact on what is happening in the moment (and why).

Of course, you have your own triggers, and you want to set up your brain to give you a trigger warning during stressful interactions. Some of your triggers will be obvious. Unfortunately, there are many more that you are unaware of, and we will attempt to find all of them throughout this guide.

Observation of Environment & Circumstance

When you interact with someone, do you ever consider the environment or the circumstances? Start paying attention to where you have meetings and those interactions that really irk you. Are they happening in the same place? Is there a theme? Where is your opponent in those meetings? Do you think your environment could have an impact on how the meetings go? I dare say, of course. A dark, gloomy room that feels cold and threatening can make you more defensive and cautious, which can then force you to give in to the other person's demands because all you could think about was how to escape that environment.

The same goes for circumstance, meaning, how did the meeting come about? Does someone always corner you or catch you at the most inopportune time? Could that be on purpose? In my experience, a lot of companies reserve the late afternoon Friday time slot to fire employees. At that time, people just want to go home and into the weekend.

They are also more likely not to make a scene for the same reason, and, as a bonus, a lot of the other employees will have left already.

Circumstance(s) could also be influencing the mental state of your opponent (or yourself). Oversleeping, being stressed, having bad interactions throughout the day, running out of coffee, worrying about bills . . . each person brings a bunch of their own circumstances to a particular circumstance within an environment.

In the earlier section "Observation of Actions," I mentioned preparedness by having imagined many other scenarios. Give some thought to the idea that another location, time, and circumstance could influence other outcomes as well. Where, when, and how you approach an interaction can give you an edge.

Forced Observations

While observation happens involuntarily, it doesn't mean that observation is always desired. School is a prime example where you read and watch an abundance of repetitive types of information. (Forced observation for the most part.)

Humanity needs forced observations. How inconducive it would be to life if we only studied what we wanted to. How would you even know if you liked something (or not) unless you touched on it somehow? School is a great place to get that first sniff of knowledge and interest. Another great example is when you have to tag along to a place or an event that is of no interest to you. I bet you have been to a home improvement store, a sporting event, a seminar, baby shower, funeral, reunion, etc. that you really didn't want to attend. Chances are someone made you—okay, asked you to—come along. Instead of dreading such experiences, see them as opportunities to watch people and to learn something new.

For me, the more I watch and observe, the more I can make sense of everything. Complicated ideas, technologies, and processes can be easier to understand in a visual context. I love watching docuseries on how things are made. Not that I'm an expert afterwards, but I can walk away with a good understanding, in this case, of the manufacturing process. When you can see how things are made, it gives you an appreciation of that product and the people behind it. It's natural for us to want to understand. Humans have a need for connection. Observation lets us make those connections.

REFLECTIONS & EXERCISES

This is where we begin to connect to the previous exercises. Having read more about observing, are there any additional points to record about your opponent that you may not have thought of previously? Let me use my Napoleon again. I want to dig a bit deeper now, so I will be more detailed in my notes. This section consists of knowledge, information, and assumptions that I have come across throughout the years.

The Napoleon

He liked **shaking everyone's hand** on first sight while making a **negative comment** about them, their work, or their environment. When people quit, he **took it personally**. When it came to raises or praise, he rarely gave them, even after promising, "If I make more money, you will too." As a business owner, he always **had the final say**, and he liked to remind everyone of that fact. At times, he was **not ethical** in his business practices (mostly in accounting principles). He was **hard to approach** or nail down for an appointment, and it seemed that he was always **on his way out** to someplace else or had something more important to do. He **loved doing fun stuff** like exploring new countries, and as such, he **didn't want to be at work** around his employees, who would distract from the attractions.

The company had been founded by **Napoleon's father, a true gentleman** who took pride not only in his work but also his employees. Napoleon's father had good standing in the industry, and he was respected and well-liked by everyone. In business, Napoleon had come to **take over his father's established company** at a fairly young age, around his midthirties. His **sisters were not involved** in the business but received money from the company on a continuous basis. Napoleon was **not on great terms with his sisters**, and they were **constantly criticizing him** about how he ran the business. His first **wife was quiet and conforming**, and she took care of the children. They eventually got divorced. There was a Chinese girlfriend, and later, an American woman whom he had met years earlier at their children's school. They married a few years ago. She **wasn't quiet or conforming**.

He **treated his property with disregard** to cleanliness, value, intactness, uniqueness. When selling his property, he would ask for as much as he had spent buying it and then got upset when people weren't biting. His **treatment of people, especially women, was not dissimilar to property**. He often made **sexist jokes** or references. He thought he was cool when he did it.

There really is a lot more, and there were consistent behaviors and experiences that resulted in my observations. I have, once again, bolded the terms that mattered most when interacting with him, and I will address these highlights in the next chapters.

The process of describing them shows that you can combine learnings and observations from personal and professional lives, acquired over a period of time, to form a good picture of who you are dealing with. You must dig in and remember. You have heard things in passing, and you have stored experiences away without much thought. Let them surface. What has this person's consistent behavior been that you can now record as facts? I'm sure there's more than what you noticed previously.

This may sound counterintuitive to my previous statement that we should not make findings with opinions or experiences in mind. However, my previous attempt to exclude influencing factors when observing was supposed to make clear that we should always consider ALL facts— not just the emotions that bubble up instantly. It is only when we are honestly reviewing all the data available to us that we can use our experiences to confirm opinions. And, once again, we must remain honest that new data can and should change our opinion if it disproves our previous standpoint. I encourage you to add additional points to your previous list of them now. If you take the time, your brain will get to the hidden observations stuck somewhere in a long-gone memory. Also, something in the future may bring forth a memory or realization of an observation about them, so make sure to be ready to hold on to what surfaces at any given time to not lose it again.

If you have done this exercise, note that while the description of them is a result based on your own experiences and knowledge, it does not explain their behavior. The description is only the bigger picture that impacts some of their behavior.

Now, let's look at one interaction with THEM in detail. Pick an interaction that had an impact on you. And let's look at it with different eyes.
Start by focusing your memory on the **ENVIRONMENT** (a.k.a. the scene). What do you remember about the day,

weather, time, location? See the setting. If outside, note the surroundings in as much detail as you can. If inside, e.g., how was the furniture arranged? Pictures on the wall, items on the desk? Temperature, lighting, sounds, or smells? Really see the event with observant eyes. Be the author who describes that place in a book. Also give some thought to where both of you were at the beginning, during, and at the end of the interaction.

Was there a special **CIRCUMSTANCE** for the interaction? Who called the meeting? Was it by chance? Do you know anything about your opponent's day or previous interactions? What was your day like before the interaction? Were you able to prepare for this meeting?

Let's move on to **APPEARANCE.** How did they dress? How did they look, smell, appear? Be as detailed as you can. You can note if anything was different (from how they usually dress/look/smell). There can be a purpose in appearances, so do not overlook this aspect. Don't forget to give yourself a good once-over. Did you wear your power suit or accessorize your outfit with something that gives you strength, like a lucky bracelet?

By first setting the scene (who's in it and where and how) while not acknowledging the action in it, you are disarming the memory. This is intentional. Take out the emotion by seeing everything that does not pertain to a human action.

Additionally, I simply want you to notice more. You've been lost in that moment like a ball in a pinball machine, getting tossed about, going wherever someone else decided. You've blocked out your senses just trying to focus on yourself in a defensive mode. Here's your chance to press that pause button and to really see. Do not get frustrated with how much or how little you recall. We are training your inner eye to start becoming more aware. Every time you try to observe/recall/rethink something, there will be a learning effect on your brain to acknowledge that effort. It will become easier with time and practice.

One more time reliving the interaction, but now I want you to focus on the ACTION (what they did), their expressions (how they looked while doing it), and their reactions (how they reacted). Also, keep in mind that it's not just them: you also had actions, expressions, and reactions. Continue to ignore the emotions.

Now we're getting into the harder part, and this is where we will do a play-by-play. Think back on who started the interaction and how. Describe (on paper or in your head) their/your actions in the scene in the order they occurred. Combined with any actions (what they or you did), you also need to determine what went along with that action. I'm referring to phrases/words that stuck out, microexpressions/body language, any visual changes (face went pale, voice raised, mouth twitched, hands interlocked, picked on scab, bad breath, firm handshake, moved behind desk, crossed arms, invaded your space, etc.).

Here's a simple example. Action: He shook my hand. Observation: held on too long, strong, sweaty palm, bad breath, leaned into my personal space. Note your reaction. Don't overcomplicate it. In the above example of a handshake that was a bit overreaching, your reaction could have been: strong handshake in return, dry palm, withdrew hand as quickly as possible, stepped backwards. As a more severe example, let's say that one of their actions was that they screamed obscenities at you. Your factual reaction could have been to leave the room or to flip them the bird. It is important to note things like, you moved to another spot, blushed, stuttered, lost your train of thought, called them a name or two, punched them, left, etc.

Really see it all as an independent observer. Do not dwell on the emotions that may come with the memory. Focus on facts and observations as the third-person point of view. We will get to the emotions in the next chapter.

Time for a break. Your brain needs to simmer on all this. Nonetheless, feel free to continue with more interactions whenever you're ready for more. And yes, it's okay to do these revivals in your head for practice.

I'm so proud of you. You are on your way to becoming a great natural observer. **Observation is the recognition of a state or the change to a (previous) state.** Why is that important? For one, observations will drive change. Additionally, our observations can lead to actions/reactions that we can anticipate or plan for, making them treasures with immense value.

CHAPTER 3: VALUE

Valuing (the verb) is a treasure.

What does that mean?

Value is something we assign to many things. We determine the worth or worthiness of something, and then we treat it accordingly. Valuing is the way you look at your world to come up with those values. In products, you value ease of use, quality, longevity, price-to-value ratio. You also value time in how it is used (or wasted), how long something (or someone) takes , how early or late something is, and how much of it may be left. If you value time, for example, then you will most likely hire a professional for a complicated home project that would take you weeks or months to complete. You value people, as in that professional who can save you time and hopefully do it with skill on top of a good price, further increasing that value. You also like some people better than others, so there is a value that you place on likability, punctuality, reliability, etc.

If you are aware of those values, then that is a great start. However, there's so much more, meaning, do you see things for what they are or for what you perceive them to be? Can you see a value in something negative or do you simply shrug it off? Are you, at times, unintentionally (or intentionally) ignoring someone's value? Can you even recognize and acknowledge what someone's value is or what it can do for you? How about your own values? How does your view of your values impact your life and your decisions? If you know your values, how do you live them every day, defend them, and use them to your advantage?

Consider that you may have been valuing everything incompletely. In this chapter, we will change the way you think about values. Valuing everything with intent is priceless to your empowerment.

Think about what you value the most. Most likely, there are things you value because they cost you a lot of money. A piece of jewelry, your car, home, children, travel, etc. And you are right to value them. They bring you joy and a sense of accomplishment.

Some of our values are expected. They are taught to us by our society, and those values connect and strengthen us, such as patriotism, religious beliefs, traditions, and commonalities in ideals. And then there's the commercial aspect, which supports societal expectations in a twisted way. Commercials are a great example in highlighting products or services that we are supposed to buy into because of an offered value or image. They paint a euphoric and an unrealistic picture of life, and they are supposed to inspire us to want more than what we have. This can leave us unhappy, incomplete, or dissatisfied with life. Take a fresh look at advertisements and consider what real value that item brings once bought. Also think about how that product is advertised and what feelings are invoked.

Of course, some products and services are truly needed, and commercials can help outline or highlight certain brands, features, and advantages. When purchasing appliances, a brand name certainly can demand a higher price. But only if that price can be supported and justified by the product's quality, longevity, ease of use, etc.

Here's the value I see in commercials: I can appreciate the creativity and smarts (or lack thereof) that a company has put into them. I love watching commercials or looking at promotional items, such as brochures, leaflets, and websites. They tell me a lot about brand consistency, messaging, style, creativity, and target audience while also allowing me a view of my world as it is perceived by the advertiser. Have you ever thought that much about advertising? The point is that this shows another approach to a value that may have been hidden before. Expand your thoughts to go beyond the value that you are expected to see.

Value is like an iceberg. There's always more than what sits on the surface.

What comes to mind when you hear the word "value"? Most of us associate value with shopping first. All the marketing tells us buy one, get one free, it's on sale, heavily discounted, bulk savings, discontinued. Value is often connected with a lesser price for a good product. We are led to believe that the deal seems so good that we'd be losing out if we didn't buy whatever was on sale. However, when products are reduced, discounted, on sale, discontinued, etc., the value lies in devaluing whatever you are buying. That's a different viewpoint. It doesn't mean that the discounted product is bad. Yet there is a reason a lesser value has now been placed on that item. There is a value and a motive for that company. They are not doing this out of the goodness of their hearts.

Women in the workplace are treated similarly. We are constantly undervalued—and a good deal for our employers—because, well, let's be honest, we let them. We become that discounted product because we are appreciative of an opportunity to build or advance our careers, and so we accept less pay as it would be pushing the envelope to ask for more. Additionally, most women will go up against—what corporations believe to be—a premium product (men), further impacting their negotiations and chances. Add to the frustration that women frequently have to prove themselves first when it comes to a potential promotion or a job, whereas men seem to get hired for jobs and/or are given promotions without any preexisting conditions.

Another item that devalues us in the workplace? Women, in an effort to connect, often volunteer too much information during interviews, reviews, and other interactions, particularly when they want something or want to make a good impression. We want to show that we have nothing to hide, highlight our talents or achievements (= our value), or explain a perceived weakness. But often, too much information comes back to bite us. Never volunteer more than what is needed to answer truthfully. You can skim around touchy points without lying. You know why? Because that potential employer or ambitious boss will do the same. Deception, such as not sharing enough information or disclosing potential downsides, is a common practice in interviews as well as in the daily workplace. Okay, deception may be too harsh; let's call it being less transparent instead. Employers pretend to be the greatest with the best culture and most flexible work environment. Most employers will disappoint. Which brings me to the next point that any job (like any relationship) is a two-way street. It's not just about what you bring to the table, but what the company offers in return in all aspects. So learn to see the value in job postings, interviews, follow-ups (or lack thereof), shared information, and job offers.

Companies and men tend to place a high value on themselves. Values that were ingrained in educational systems, religious organizations, and governments (society and culture). I don't want to imply that men haven't worked hard individually to get to where they are. But we cannot deny that life has been much easier for (white) men to help them understand and maintain their role in society as expected leaders and providers.

What is a woman's value then? Women's expected values were also indoctrinated in educational systems, religious organizations, and governments (society and culture). The exclusion of women or limited scope of allowed inclusion can say a lot about how a society values women. Some say that our value is only as much as someone else is willing to see in us (or pay us for). I'm going to call BS on that.

Let's start with you. Your value is unique to you. You single-handedly need to determine your worth/value and then come up with certainties (which are your non-negotiables in life) and boundaries that will protect you from being worth less and worthless. These are your core values. Mind you, a lot of other values can change depending on an opportunity, but your certainties and boundaries should not diminish.

For example, for the right job opportunity, I would consider less money if some of the other benefits could rise to the occasion, such as life-work balance, future opportunities, and offered health benefits. However, my certainties and boundaries would still apply: freedom to operate and authority (not just responsibilities). Here's another viewpoint (when faced with an absence of one of my core values): If I cannot impact change, or better said, if I am not allowed to impact change, then I cannot and will not work for a company no matter how much money I make. This freedom to operate is where I draw my line; it's a must and a non-negotiable. Now that doesn't mean that I would sacrifice my salary. For a certain role at a certain size company, and based on my experience and academics, I expect to be paid fairly.

When I'm on a job hunt, I pay attention to a lot of things, like how self-centered the job posting has been written (as in, it's all about their requirements, their must-haves, the endless list of job duties, etc. while not providing information about what they offer, their culture, their benefits, etc.), how a hiring manager talks and listens (tone, style, energy), what is or is not being said, when and how the follow-up happens, how transparent the communication is, etc.

I can recognize a value that is presented to me, and I can recognize a value that I offer in return. Let me give you an example of how I approached values in a past job interview. I had been contacted by a German business owner who wanted to grow the U.S. side of her business. She had taken over the management of her company from her father, and she was still young (younger than me) and seemed hesitant about a few things. She did not feel like she had many allies. In the U.S., she had hired a male general manager to get things set up (from the German HQ originally), but after a few years, this person quit and started a competing company. His company grew into a much more successful business in the States than hers, and she felt betrayed by him. I had run small German companies in the past, and having a former ex-employee work at this competitor—and hence knowing the culture of the all-male club there—this job had piqued my interest. I knew that this bunch of guys worked extremely well together; they were all young when they started the company, and they were hungry. In talking with her, I saw us as a female powerhouse to conquer the American market away from the boys. We had some great conversations about trust and female leadership, and we both stated our interest in working together.

I prepared a rough proposal on how I envisioned her business to succeed in the U.S. When we talked the next time, she said that she was hesitant to make any big hiring decisions without having met me in person. This was right after the beginning of the COVID-19 pandemic. I told her that I understood, I was employed and not desperate for another job, and that we could talk again when she was ready. A few days later, she requested another call. I was surprised but even more so when she proposed the following: Seeing that she couldn't make the big hiring decision from afar, would I be interested in starting out as an inside sales representative for X amount of money, which would give me an opportunity to learn about the company's products and processes while also getting to know the team? Additionally, she could get a feel for who I was as a person, and then when things went back to normal (no travel restrictions), she could potentially move me up to the general manager position.

Sound reasonable?

Absolutely not.

This suggestion shows the hard truth and ugliness about what's wrong with women's values in the professional world.

I'm convinced that hiring managers would not make this suggestion to any man in a top-level management position. Most men would be offended if they would have to prove themselves first in a lesser position. A man knows his value (even if his value is overstated), and he typically is not challenged by potential employers in his representation. I had run multiple manufacturing facilities in my past successfully. I had come highly recommended to her. Yet she still refused to see my value. She was stuck on distrust from former male subordinates and how they had screwed her over. Furthermore, being a woman had taught her that settling is the norm and acceptable. To add insult to injury, the offered salary was laughable, there were no benefits to speak of, and my commute would have been horrific.

I wasn't quite as politically correct in my answer to her as I could have been. Because she is part of the problem, and I needed her to know this. She put distrust above all her decisions, she clung to the past, and she was not willing to move forward due to her insecurities.

I have worked hard all my life, proving myself to others. I had shown what I could do. My results spoke volumes. And I was, and still am, unwilling to lower my value solely because someone is unable to acknowledge it with a fair amount of pay, respect, and authority. Furthermore, I will not pay (be held accountable) for another person's previous mistakes. I'm not them. Her company and the potential of a GM position no longer had any value to me. I had gone in interviewing for the GM position, not an inside sales job. What was she thinking? Yet it happens to women all the time.

I don't want to work for someone who doesn't trust me or the world. Who thinks they can offer me less because they feel that they are taking a huge risk hiring me. There's so much selfishness in that thought. The risks are always higher for the candidate, not the company.

Another thing I know for certain: I would have never had her respect if I had taken the lower position (or her employees' respect who would have known me as a peer first, which is never a good path). If I would have allowed her to walk all over my worth, anything going forward would have been lost energy, a disservice to my fellow women, and a disgrace to the women who have fought so hard for women's rights. Accepting the job under these conditions would have set the tone for all interactions going forward. And that tone would have been one of submission and acceptance of worthlessness. There would be no way for me to impact any change at her company. It was most likely the reason why her former GM had left. He probably had not been allowed to manage as freely as he had wanted or imagined. Her trust issues were massive.

I also want you to note that, in a job interview, it is your duty to ask some harder questions if you want to find out how your potential future boss or company could react to pressure or conflict. Here's a great opportunity to hone your listening skills. In my example above, while I tried to be forthcoming as an interested candidate, she was trying to bully me into accepting the lesser job once she encountered my resistance. She kept pointing out all the benefits (most of them hers). And when I finally pushed back, she went silent. It wasn't surprising. Not because the tone and honesty of my pushback were strong, but because I had figured by then that she was so insecure in her trust issues, that she would take offense to my email. She was afraid and intimidated and not used to a strong female voice. I would never want to have her as my boss.

The consensus should not be that women are content to settle for less. We must stop accepting those attempts to demote and devalue ourselves for someone else's benefit. People and companies that don't value YOU, don't deserve you.

I'm glad that my experiences, especially the bad ones, have opened my eyes to see my value and to stand up for it when someone wants to tread on it. In parts, I have been able to do this thanks to my financial independence.

The Value of Financial Independence
At the risk of sounding like a broken record, I can't stress the value of financial independence enough. Maybe you're just intimidated because overcoming financial dependence is a tremendous task. Truth is, it would have been

impossible for me to turn down a disadvantageous job offer if I were financially unstable and/or struggling.

When you are loaded up with debt, you will be committed to a job with a certain salary requirement to simply sustain. Speaking from experience, you will not get far in your pursuit of personal freedom or transformation if you are shackled to debt that is out of control. Everything you aim to do is harder when you cannot make decisions based on your freedom to choose your employer. It's not about being employed that should drive you but about you deciding who you will work for.

This can be a hard pill to swallow. Especially if you are reading this because you want to get away from a bad job environment, and you have debt that prevents you from leaving on your terms (when and how). Companies love employees who are in debt up to their eyeballs. This ensures that they must come to work. Chances are they are willing to work overtime. They will be too busy or too exhausted, not to mention overwhelmed with their daily lives, to look for a better job or company. It also allows companies to treat their employees with less value. Financially (and emotionally) struggling employees will do anything or agree to anything to simply keep their jobs. Think about it: Who has control over you when you keep piling on debt, when you keep wasting money on things you don't need and maybe later realize haven't added any value to your personal well-being? At what cost?

How did I achieve financial independence? Slowly. When I decided somewhere in my corporate career that I wanted to write a book about "The Dick Club," I realized that I couldn't write it while employed. There just wasn't enough time or energy in the day. I decided to either give up on my dream or to start making moves toward achieving it. Remember how I addressed keeping your dreams and ambitions top of mind in the LEARN chapter? I decided to move forward as I still felt very passionate about women's rights. I settled on a timeline ("I'm going to quit my job to start a book in five years"), and I shifted into DRIVE. Each paycheck, I allocated as much as I could toward reducing my debt. It was slow going at first. I made good money, but I paid a fortune each month on health insurance for my husband and me. I decided to look for another job. There was no urgency in finding the next best offer with more money. I searched methodically to find a job that fit my specific skill set, offered fair pay, and covered more of the health insurance premiums. Timing was great, and within a few months, I had an offer from a German company aligning with my requirements. It wasn't more money necessarily in salary, but the savings in health insurance premiums every month were over a thousand dollars. That's a lot of money to put toward debt. Granted, my husband and I did not have an overabundance of debt, but the principle is the same.

I also didn't splurge or overextend my credit. No fancy vacations, no large exuberant purchases, and I limited my online shopping to the items that I really needed. Every purchase was a conscious and honest decision. My husband and I never bought into the American dream of having a large house that would mean a big mortgage for thirty years. You can make a lot of money and still struggle financially. Both of us have learned that we value our time over material showpieces, and we'd rather retire early with less income. You do not need a large nest egg if you live small and smart. Expensive tangible exteriors do not guarantee a happy interior. Once our debt was gone (years later), I focused on saving money. I had never planned on or asked for my husband's financial support. He would have given it, but it was important for me to do this on my own terms financially. I did not intend to strain our marriage by him paying all our monthly expenses while I stayed home typing away on a book that would not produce any income for years (or ever). I had always budgeted my money and kept a tally on my income and expenses, so I knew how much I needed every month to sustain our lifestyle. It took about eight years from the first thought to quitting my job, and then, I wrote my book. (For those of you counting the years, I stated eight years since my first thought of writing the book. I remained in the neutral stage for years until I committed to the cause with a timeline. That's three years of talk and no action. Once I made the commitment and a plan on how to achieve my financial freedom, I was able to meet my deadline. Nonetheless, it could have taken me longer. Getting there is the real goal; meeting a deadline is just a bonus.)

Depending on your life and circumstances, there is always a way. But it will take dedication, commitment, and a plan. Not to mention an attitude that says that it is possible. If you feel discouraged, don't be. You must start somewhere. The sad thing would be if you look back after eight years and realize what could have been if you would have just taken that first step.

The Value of Failure

Life happens while we make our plans. Keep in mind that plans should be fluid; they should change or adapt if your new circumstance warrants it. This includes what you perceive to be failures. Not achieving a goal, failing to complete a task, losing a job, not getting the promotion, sucking at a hobby. These are not failures but merely chances to pivot and adapt (and adjust). Every perceived failure is an opportunity to try something new or different as well as to learn something about yourself. You can shape your life even when you don't feel like you have control. You do. Others may impact your circumstance, but ultimately, you are in control over what you decide to do next.

Every bad decision I have made in my life has resulted in the person I am today, whom I love. I wouldn't want to change a thing about where I am or what I represent. Every misstep along the way has helped me to understand myself better because I was also (eventually) willing to learn and observe (and value), which led to empowerment. No regrets. It is important to take the next step and accept your decisions, as good or as bad as they turn out to be. You will be okay. You can pivot and adapt and make the best of any situation. You've done it so far. Now you can do it with more awareness and appreciation.

Additionally, think of failure as a great equalizer. It reminds us to remain humble. That is a good thing. Have you met those (sometimes arrogant) people who succeed at anything they try the very first time? They make it look easy and natural. Do you think they appreciate what they have as much as that person who has tried and failed and tried again? Furthermore, let's acknowledge that someone else's definition of success or failure can never be the same as yours. It's impossible. There is no standard that defines failure or success, only expectations, and you should have learned by now that we are done trying to fit into a mold made by others.

Failure, simply put, is honesty. It will show you what to improve before you succeed.

The Value of Ambitions and/or a Skill Set

Here's where you need to learn to value and balance your knowledge, your ambition, your academics, your experience, and your happiness. Realize what you are good at, where there is a need in the job market for your strengths, what jobs interest you, what your ultimate professional goal is, or how you can turn a passion into something tangible—all while keeping your physical and mental happiness top of mind. Do you know where you want to be in life in general? In five years? When you want to retire and how? If you haven't thought about it, now is the time. Take control of steering yourself in the direction of your end goal. Be honest in your assessment.

For example, what would it take to land your dream job? A college degree or experience with the right level of skill set? Let's talk about the elephant on campus. No doubt, for some careers, a degree is a must. Certain subjects cannot be taught anywhere other than on a college campus (in person or online). It can be a personal choice, though, when a degree is not required for a career you want to pursue. Additionally, it is not the key to happiness and financial success. The debt one can incur when attending college can have a lasting impact on every decision made thereafter. Yes, money is your key to financial freedom, but you don't need a lot to be free of limitations. It's a bit of a contradiction, but chances are, if you go to college, you will take on a lot of debt. And even though you may get a job that pays well, it may not free you from financial burden, especially if you are buying into the expectations of the American dream, as in a big house with a huge mortgage, fancy furnishings, a car to go along with your status, and a few kids who will represent additional financial hurdles.

I never felt that a college degree would have resulted in the best version of me as I moved up the corporate ladder. Granted, it would have added to my leadership skills and business acumen, but it wasn't worth the return on the investment to me. In consideration of the cost and the associated debt in relation to my age and my plans for my future, I did not value it to be of value to me personally. In the companies that I managed, my strengths were my street smarts and the perseverance that came from working my way up based on spite. I achieved success because I was willing to learn what was needed to get the job done. Not because of what other people perceived a college degree to represent. I have not seen, in my experience, that a college degree guaranteed profits or ethics. I have seen a lot of talent wasted because college graduates leaned heavily on academia while abandoning common sense. There's got to be reasoning.

Another important point is knowing what impact you want to have on others and what tools are necessary to achieve that impact. While a college degree would have made me more attractive to potential large employers, it was ultimately not my goal to work for a big company. I've always thought of large corporations as part of a larger profit system that does not recognize or value individuals. I never wanted to be one of many. I had dreamed of making the big bucks, no doubt. In the end, though, I was honest with myself. The price tag of selling my soul and my values to profits and shareholders was too steep. I loved working with small start-up companies where I could make an actual difference. Granted, I was working to help someone else profit higher up, but private business owners are often less greedy and do see their employees as part of a larger family. I mattered to the people at the bottom of that food chain who desperately needed good management. For that, I didn't need a college degree. I have a great skill set in that I can be hands-on while managing, and that particular talent is mostly needed at start-ups or small companies that value managers who can jump in and do it all. Still, I had to make peace with the fact that I would never earn as much. Plus, I would have to work a lot harder for less pay (being a woman had already given me that experience, so no news there).

It is a decision I consciously made and maintain. It is a decision that, to this day, gets me thrown out of every upper management application asking for a college degree. And these days, a lot of companies expect you to have at least an associate's degree even for entry level jobs (or so it seems). It hasn't discouraged me though; I keep applying to larger organizations if I feel that I could really change things up or when a job posting sounds more inclusive or fun. I apply for the sake of seeing if someone can look beyond an expectation or a mold. It's been quiet thus far, and I don't fret over the exclusion. Ultimately, I know where I can do my best work, and that is with those who have even less of a voice than my own: the blue-collar workers on the manufacturing floor. I am good at representing their needs and wants, and I always had a positive impact on my company's culture by fighting for their rights. Healthy change starts from the bottom up.

Knowing your skill set combined with what you want to accomplish professionally and personally, should determine a path for you where you can sustain your finances, lifestyle, and happiness. A word on happiness: Pursue a career that offers what you seek internally and externally. When you're happy with your job, work takes on a new meaning. I love working because I don't view it as work but as an opportunity to improve. Additionally, I stand behind my decision of having accepted employment, and I commit to a positive attitude and the job at hand. This upbeat energy and approach transfers to others, causing a ripple effect. Imagine that you can be the reason why others enjoy coming to work. That's a huge motivator for me. Everyone is drawn to positivity. The best part is that positive energy will help you gain allies.

The Value of Faking It

Lately, I have seen a lot of comments that put down the term "fake it till you make it." There's nothing wrong with faking it until you make it, in my opinion. Nobody knows about your insecurities unless you clue them in. If you don't know if you should apply for a job because you lack a skill, then you must know that you can learn that skill and that you don't have to lie about it in your application process.

But you don't have to embellish it either. If you can learn or are willing to learn whatever that shortcoming is, then you can sell that in the way you represent yourself. Draw on similar past challenges, and show them how you have overcome other perceived weaknesses. Never beg (as in, "If you give me a chance, I will do anything, pretty please"). Be assertive instead: "I don't see any issues with me getting up to speed on XYZ. At ABC company, I quickly . . ." Show an example of your tenacity. Show them results and successes. And while the lack of a skill may result in a lower salary, you should make it clear that you expect a bump later based on your performance, before you accept. Project strength, calmness, and determination, and do not falter when someone questions your abilities. If you don't get the job, it wasn't meant to be.

Men fake so much better than women when it comes to jobs, as discussed earlier in this chapter. Yet, as women, haven't we always faced all challenges thrown our way? We can fake our way to a better job (most women have faked orgasms, so let's draw from that!). We have overcome so much in our lives. Women continually learn what is needed to survive, and so we will always land on our feet. Do not be afraid of what you don't know. Be excited that you get to learn something new. Faking it simply means believing in yourself. You can do this. If a man can, it's no big deal.

Faking it doesn't mean lying. Say you did get that job; then it's okay to share with others that you will need help. That shows humility and willingness to include others for input. One of my strengths is to draw from my team's combined knowledge and experience, and I acknowledge everyone who makes an effort to contribute. As a unit, a team can deal with anything successfully if they know they are valued and included.

The Value of Honesty, Confrontation,
No-Apologies, and Boundaries

Honesty, confrontation, no-apologies, and boundaries are four awesome self-care items that can be combined into one incredible value: Everyone can appreciate knowing where they stand. There's a ton of value in not having to play games because it lets you be your authentic self. Others will adjust to you because you have made it very clear to them what you represent. However, most of you will have a problem with real authenticity. It's so much easier to conform, to give in, to be compliant. Being authentic means that you are true to yourself and all your beliefs. At first glance, you think you are . . . but are you really? Practicing these four self-care items will be tough initially, but the results will speak volumes down the road. I appreciate and respect people who are assertive and authentic. Even when those people are Dicks. I respect honesty in authenticity, and I can deal with them in an uncomplicated way.

Honesty's value is in not having to worry about keeping up a lie. Honesty results in a clean conscience. It's about integrity. You can look in the mirror at the end of the day without guilt. You and others will value knowing that what you say or do (or don't do) matters. It is important to know where you stand and for others to acknowledge that. Honesty will attach a high value to you as a coworker, boss, friend, and mentor—and to yourself.

Honesty is also important when it comes to confrontations. Addressing issues, concerns, hurdles, problems, complaints, challenges, goals, etc. with honesty will get to solutions much quicker than letting these fester and grow into even bigger problems. For example, when confronted, don't try to cover up a mistake you have made, especially when it will help rectify a solution quickly. Your boss, coworkers, family, friends, etc. will appreciate that time has not been wasted, and as a bonus, this behavior will give you integrity, respect, and believability going forward. The same goes for inappropriate or bad behavior. It is totally okay to admit when you are out of line or wrong about something. Do it in that moment, and it will help simmer down tempers. You will feel in control more and more the sooner you confront a problem and your honesty. If you don't, this problem will eat at you, and it will continue to do so until you face it. I can't think of anyone going to bed happy about an ongoing, pestering issue. Quite the opposite. I think it's more stressful allowing the situation to continue than it is to address it.

Setting boundaries and foregoing apologies will result in a less stressed version of yourself while building up your confidence. For example, people will think twice about dumping work on you that is not within your area of responsibility or that would unfairly impact your working conditions and overall performance. A simple, "I have a deadline to meet on XYZ, that does not allow me to take on additional tasks. Maybe you can approach ABC to see how priorities can be reorganized," is good enough while also offering a solution on next steps. There is no need to apologize about being busy with another project. Why would you? You don't make your workload, so you are not responsible for not having time. It will be up to your boss to decide which project has the higher priority. And if it is your boss dumping additional work on you, then you need to explain how added tasks will impact other projects and your performance. You are setting up a framework for your rules of engagement, which will shape how people interact with you going forward. They will know that they can't approach you without reason or due process. Of course, a company could fire you if you continually refuse an added workload, but you must determine your value first and prioritize yourself and your mental and physical health ahead of the company's failure to implement better processes. Remember the saying: your lack of planning does not constitute a crisis on my part (all the time). We all are willing to take on more at work under the right circumstances (such as increased pay, chance of a promotion, recognition, pride in workmanship and accomplishment, team morale, etc.). It's a two-way street—always. Job descriptions are subject to change, but when the goalpost gets moved by a mile, there should be reciprocation in benefits to you.

With any of these self-care items, words matter, spoken and written, and your goal must be to be nice—to a point. However, you don't have to take on the burden of being nice for the wrong reasons or when it's not warranted. Especially in business, it's all about getting something accomplished in an efficient way so as not to waste time, effort, and false pretenses while showing yourself to be confident in your presentation. Stating a fact (without attaching emotion to it) that can hurt someone's feelings is a must sometimes. Again, if you must point out something negative or address someone's weakness, then we must also point to the positives before offering support to correct such issues.

All the above will make you feel less responsible for other people's feelings. That is not a horrible thing. Think about it. Ultimately, you cannot feel responsible or be held responsible for how someone feels about themselves. Everyone lives their own lives, and as such, everyone is responsible for themselves, including their feelings. Once you realize that, it will take a load off. We must be considerate of others' feelings, of course. But you cannot control and should never try to control how someone feels about themselves, especially if they have caused whatever harm is now coming their own way. If someone's been a Dick, karma will find them eventually. I do want to acknowledge that I'm not asking you to act like one in return. Let's exclude that behavior (as that would put partial blame on you for their feelings). I'm assuming that you are the type of person who dreads giving bad news. You are empathetic, and you do not want to hurt anyone's feelings. There's a right and a wrong way to share negative feedback (objectivity is the key), and if you keep the focus on improvement and encouragement, I promise this will not be horrible.

The Value of Knowledge

When you know, you know. And when you don't know, you know. There's so much power and confidence in being knowledgeable. Knowledge makes you a good leader, mentor, teacher, and role model. Knowledge will broaden your horizons, allow for critical thinking, and help you make good decisions. Knowledge is supported by facts (most of the time). I'm super confident when I head into meetings where I know the subject matter. I don't worry about debating my points; I'm viewed as an expert who can be relied on by others. Additionally, even when I'm not super knowledgeable about something, I know that I can learn. I'm not afraid to ask questions. I'm honest about my knowledge. I don't have to make up anything or lie. People will respect you more for being honest about insufficient knowledge, even admire you for admitting it. They will also value you because you value other people's knowledge, especially if you are inclusive at work, drawing on combined knowledge from the entire team.

I also value what I know about people. That includes my observations. Realizing the depth of that knowledge is important when it comes to our interactions. Because all my knowledge—the accumulation of all the data (about me, them, the environment, the facts, the circumstances, the values, objectives, etc.)—will help me steer my interactions toward positive outcomes.

What else do I value about knowledge? The obvious: We will never know it all. That is human. That fact can get you down at times. But don't let it. Knowledge takes time, and it doesn't have an end point—there are just different levels. The good news? Our limits are movable. How valuable!

The Value of Information

This is different from the value of knowledge. Information does not automatically translate to knowledge. Information can be anything: gossip, rumors, hearsay, assumptions, theories, truths, lies . . . and it remains as such unless we can associate facts. When you come across new information, you must determine if it's knowledge or trash. Consider the sources, the intent, the creator, and the presentation or framework. What value does it have to the creator/publisher? What are they trying to achieve? Information can be full of fake news disguised as science. Treat information as information that is mostly useless when interacting with others. The power and value lie in information that has been transformed into knowledge through factual observations and experiences. However, it says something about another person's value (to you) if they are judging or acting purely from information, not knowledge. There is value in knowing the difference and in who is using which one at any given time.

The Value of Leaving

This applies to a bad relationship or job. Leaving can be so freeing. Yet often, we are too afraid to head into the unknown. I am a prime example, having stayed with an abusive drunk for five years. Fear of not knowing where to go, what to do, what will come next. It can be debilitating. I felt so cut off from everything. My entire family was in Germany, and during those times, calling internationally cost a fortune. There were no social media or other communication apps. I could not imagine a way out. Shame is another reason that keeps women with their abusers and/or in a bad work environment. I had shame. My parents had told me that my marriage was a bad decision. I didn't want to admit that they had been right. Nobody wants to be told, "I told you so."

In my situation, it took a long time to realize how far I had come without any help. I had left my home country and moved into a strange land, not knowing how life worked there. My (then) husband offered no support. I had no value to him other than to cook, clean, and please him sexually. And when he broke down during his drinking rampages, sobbing about his poor life, he relied on me to be his emotional handkerchief. Despite that, I had managed so much on my own. I found a job, and I had maneuvered through American bureaucracies and life in a foreign country on my own. I had gotten raises, which meant that my employer saw more value in me than my own spouse, who was calling me four times per day to ensure I wasn't mingling with my coworkers. I was proud that I had taken charge of the household finances while also maintaining my own separate bank account. There was success in my struggles, but I was afraid of him. I worried that on the escalation scale, his verbal and emotional abuse would eventually lead to physical abuse, which was a common practice in the area we lived in.

Reading a book on codependency and having encouraging coworkers (one who offered up her couch if I decided to leave), finally made me see how the unknown could not be worse than what I was going through every single day. I knew I had strength, resilience, and stubbornness. I knew I could make it no matter what the world was going to throw at me, after what I had endured. And I wondered what my life could be like without such a limiting factor in it. The unknown can be the best thing you can flee to. Routine is your enemy in bad situations. Routine, in that sense, translates to a false sense of comfort and safety. Comfort in knowing what we have and will experience (and are willing to experience), not comfort in sense and body. A routine will keep you stagnant. Breaking out will be empowering. There is always a greater value in leaving a bad relationship or job than in staying.

When it comes to my past jobs, I have always left on my terms. This makes me a lucky person, but not all of it has to do with luck. I am confident in my ability to succeed in any job based on my past success, and I enjoy learning new industries, products, and processes. With every new job in my life, I have learned so much about myself and others. This does not mean that I would recommend quitting your job frequently. But when you quit, do so with purpose to better yourself. Of course, it's best to hang on to your current job until you have something new lined up if you are not financially independent.

It is also totally okay to pursue a new job temporarily if that job will get you closer to your goals. It may not be your dream job. Most likely, it will not be, and on top of it, there will be some negatives. No job is ever perfect. But if that job offers you that ONE thing that will accelerate you down that road to your success, then suck it up a few years (or months) and do it. You may come across a job that offers needed experience or exposure to elevate you in your field of expertise. Use a job until you can reach the next level. Something negative can be of value if you make use of it with intent and purpose.

The Value of a Toxic Relationship

What possible value could come out of a toxic relationship? You'd be surprised. In the five years that I stayed married to my verbally abusive alcoholic, I was focused on taking care of him by way of appeasement. His abuse made me an expert in reading and anticipating emotions. When your survival or your physical and mental health depend on keeping your opponent in check, then you are good at recognizing triggers. You've become the authority on this person, and you know exactly what to do (or not to do) to ensure that they stay within limits. In a way, you are manipulating that person to avoid confrontation, escalation, or bodily harm. While it is not the best way to learn about triggers, it is one of the fastest. Any long-term toxic relationship will make you an expert at reading other people's emotions. But you may have not used this "gift" when your senses are not on high alert (as in, outside of survival mode).

Acknowledgment is another value. I had avoided it for years. I did not want to admit that my life was a mess, and that it was all my fault. I felt shame. Sure, I had known for a while (probably years, or even from the start) that the relationship was more damaging than mutually beneficial. Sometimes, we're not ready to acknowledge because it hurts to disappoint. Not just ourselves but also our families and friends. Acknowledgment is about moving forward and out of that toxic relationship. Defeat in this sense is a win. Acknowledgment is knowing that you have given this relationship your all, and there is no more. It also acknowledges that blame and shame have no place in the equation when it comes to life or death. Blaming and shaming ourselves are part of our codependence. Codependence is all about someone else needing us, or us thinking they need us, and us prioritizing our life around them to benefit and help them. It is the furthest from self-care that you can get. Codependence has its roots in feeling responsible for other people's feelings. Some people cannot be helped. Some people don't deserve your empathy and loyalty.

Learn from your toxic relationships, including the professional ones. In theory, you don't ever have to make the same mistake again if you are willing to be observant from the get-go and draw from your past experiences. You can recognize the symptoms and the behaviors that do not align with your values. Your gut also tends to have the right instinct, and it will be the first to send up warning flares. Worst case, and there's value in that: you can escape again if you find yourself in another toxic relationship. Value that you have persevered in the past, and marvel at how strong you are because of it. A toxic relationship will show you how resilient, smart, adaptive, intuitive, and stubborn you are. You can face anything. You can count on yourself. Do you know how valuable that is?

The Value of Support

Every good relationship is a two-way street, and as such, it likely won't last if only one party contributes. Hopefully, you have a tribe that supports you and that you support. I may have stayed with my alcoholic a lot longer if it weren't for a group of former coworkers who encouraged me to move on. The most important support came from a colleague who offered up her couch for several months until I could land on my feet financially. In return, I babysat her children.

Most tasks and goals can happen faster and easier with the right support system. Sure, I could have achieved my book goal without the support of my current husband, but why? He was there to help me in whatever capacity. He was willing to give me more than I would have ever asked for. Sharing goals and struggles are vital in sustaining relationships and your support system. You have friends, coworkers, bosses, and people you don't even know who are rooting for you. They would be willing to help and support. Are you aware of these options? Find and make use of your support system. Sometimes, those who you think you can count on will fail you. And sometimes, those you never think of will come through big. My husband is at the core of my support system, as are several close friends. I make sure that I offer and give support in return. Those tight relationships are the most important ones in my life, and I strive to nourish and value them. All women have stories of abuse, personal or professional. You have allies. You can find them. Who can you count on? Do they know it? Don't be afraid to ask.

At work, your support could also come from the human resources department. However, HR managers can be under a lot of stress as the go-between for corporations and the people working in them. This often means that employees' voices go unnoticed because HR is more concerned with pleasing the higher-ups than presenting conflict. It takes incredible leadership at the highest level of a company to be inclusive and to want to work on interpersonal problems through all departments. Sometimes, the HR manager is merely a figure of pretend. Other times, HR is truly empowered to offer support. Just be aware that it may take a while to figure out if HR is an ally or a foe. My advice is that I would always approach HR with caution until their actions show how valuable of a resource they can be (or not). An HR manager with ethics, morals, and business sense will do the right thing for the employees and not side with management on everything. As allies, they will support and guide you and the company toward solutions. As foes, they will add to the complexity of your challenges at work.

Here's a support aid that you may have never thought of: If your company has an employee handbook, there should be guidelines on general expected behaviors (attendance, dress code, sick days, etc.) as well as an outline on how to deal with and report issues. I bet whenever someone disobeyed the rules, management has thrown this book at them. It can be interesting to see them squirm when you use their policies to invoke your rights as an employee. However, handbooks often have the bare minimum employee protections in mind while enforcing the mentality of corporate oppression. Nonetheless, no manager will be able to deny written processes that the company has declared as their own set of rules. So make sure to read your handbook. (If some of the policies are vague, you can also use that to your advantage. Policies that are ambiguous will always work in your favor.)

The Value of a Great Teacher/Mentor

I've had some awesome mentors. They crossed my path as if by accident. I didn't give them much thought at first. They made learning so inclusive and normal. They inspired me to be better and to reach for the stars. Sometimes, you don't see the value of a great teacher until you come across a horrible one. When I had looked at riding lessons in Germany, I was appalled. The instructor yelled at the students the entire lesson, telling them what they did wrong. I can't recall one positive. Who wants that? How much can you learn from someone who only sees the negatives? Just because you know something well enough to teach it, does not justify you belittling the ones who come looking for that knowledge.

Remember that I had mentioned in the LEARN chapter that not all teachers are experts? That is true. Nonexperts can be scammers, simply out for your money. They're faking it in the worst way, without intent to make good on their promises. Yet nonexperts can also be incredible teachers. Think of your parents, artists, athletes, friends, or other people you have admired for a characteristic, skill, behavior, talent, etc. They may lack scholastic achievements in their field of specialty, but they have more than made up for any shortcomings through other avenues: tenacity, learning by doing, pure will, new approaches, life experiences, etc. They are the proof that success is never out of reach. A mentor's value is that they will enable you to progress faster and with purpose. They will teach you the shortcuts or details, be part of your support system, and empower without prejudice. Mentors/teachers are your biggest cheerleaders and allies. A huge bonus? Good teachers are good confrontationists. Their goal is to get to the root of any weaknesses so that you can succeed. And their approach to any challenge will be inclusive and positive.

Mentorship can also give you a renewed appreciation of your trade, talent, or skill. It can show you how far you have come, and you can be that role model to someone else.

The Value of Emotions

When I mentioned earlier in this chapter that we are not responsible for other people's feelings, this does not mean that we should shut out or shun observing and feeling emotions on ourselves and others. Emotions have an immense value when it comes to recognizing triggers. The key is to become aware of those emotions that develop into triggers to a certain behavior, with the hardest part being the observation and acknowledgment of emotions without emotions.

Take yourself for starters. Once you can identify an emotion in a certain setting with a certain person, then, at that point, you can connect the emotion to an action or reaction. The larger the emotion, then the larger the chances that there is an emotional trigger that just got activated. That trigger will make you respond in a predictable manner, and that is a pattern of behavior unique to you. You need this conscious coupling of emotion and trigger so that you can use it to turn off your emotions to avoid the triggers. By turning the emotions off, I don't want to imply that we ignore them. Not exactly, but yes. You want to acknowledge the emotion to become aware of the trigger. Acknowledging the emotion *now* will turn into putting that emotion on the back burner *later* to make way for a more controlled response. We all know what happens when emotions take over. Things escalate quickly. Nothing gets accomplished when emotions run high.

This is also helpful when observing others. If someone has an outburst, then that person was triggered by a preceding action. Try watching conflict interactions from afar as it will allow you to be less emotional. Once you observe emotions more factually, then you will also understand that nothing is personal. People can't help themselves when their emotions take over. They tend to go on the offensive or defensive. Never take anything personally when interacting with an emotional opponent. Words are controlled by emotions, and sometimes, in the heat of the argument, things are being said because that person has lost their ability to think clearly and factually, and all they can resort to are insults. Viewing others with pity—because they could not control themselves—can offer deflection (the focus is on them, not your own feelings). Meaning, in that moment, focus your attention on them versus trying to figure out how YOU feel about them (insulting you). Really see all their signals (facial and body expressions, gestures, noise level, word choices, etc.). If instead, you are solely focusing on how you feel, you will miss the opportunity to take charge of what happens next. See that these people don't hate you; they just don't know how to deal with the emotions that you have stirred up. If that happens, celebrate the fact that you can recognize what just happened.

That recognition of emotions and triggers will make you feel very empowered and in control. The value lies in being able to read your opponent (and yourself). And this will lead to changed actions and reactions driven by you. Valuing emotions will give you the upper hand in controlling the outcome.

Think about it. If you are not aware of the emotions (especially your opponent's) and things escalate to where they run amok, then you're not getting anything accomplished and you're definitely not making friends. This means that you lost any benefit that could have come out of the interaction. That's especially sad if you had a specific purpose. Both of you are going to walk away from this interaction drained and frustrated. Furthermore, all future interactions are now compromised. That is not what we want. Valuing emotions keeps us on track. And they show that other people do have feelings, as inhumane as they may appear.

When we get to the final chapter, EMPOWER, that's where you'll get to experience the value of emotions, because our goal is to exclude them from our decisions. While we value emotions, they only serve one purpose when we want to empower ourselves: they are our trigger warnings.

The Value of YOU

Priceless. Okay, your value is for you to decide. It may also change depending on circumstances. But in its core, you know what you stand for and where your boundaries are. You must stick to being you. When it comes to interactions (but really anything), you must know going in what you value the most; it's the one thing you must protect and keep top of mind. For example, if you go into a meeting with your boss who is trying to gather information about a coworker for a performance review, and they ask about rumors/gossip, trying to badger you into talking badly about this person, then you must stand up for yourself and that person by refusing to join in on the trash talk—that is, if one of your core values is not lying (and decency). This value is your most precious treasure in any interaction besides the other objectives set for that meeting. Other emotions cannot override—such as your desire to please your boss. The value that is uniquely you is also a combination of your upbringing, your academics, your experiences, your skills, your knowledge, etc., and you must be aware of what you bring to the table at all times. Keep learning. Knowing your values will make all your decisions easier. But you must also value those values.

What are you risking by not knowing your values? Let me redirect for clarity. Have you ever had a friend who, when she got into a new relationship, completely disappeared from your life? Your friend is crazy about this new person, and she wants to spend every minute with them. However, it is easy to see that this new relationship is not a healthy one, and she is starting to lose herself in it. At first, when you hang out, this new lover will come along and pretend to be your best friend. Then, slowly but surely, there will be conflicts and cancellations for future get-togethers because her new partner has (obvious-to-you) trust issues. On the rare occasion you talk on the phone, there's a huge wall that has never been there before. You fear to address your concerns. She seems happy. You don't want to be the friend to question her happiness, even when it's fake. Losing friendships because of a new relationship is bad for both parties. You don't ever want to be that friend to someone by being too focused on a new relationship and forgetting about who you are as a person. Yet, despite our best intentions, suppressing our values can happen more easily and without us noticing at first. If you have not established your values (and live them), and if you do not practice self-care, you will lose yourself in a new relationship with a selfish person. A partner is a complement—not the only value-add to make you more worthy. The same applies to a job.

Most people who have healthy, lasting, and thriving relationships are quite comfortable in their own skin. They could live by themselves, they are not afraid to spend time with themselves, and they don't see a relationship or a job as the saving grace to validate them as a better person (or to deflect from their inner demons). If you find yourself going from one relationship or job to the next without skipping a beat (time for yourself), then something is off in your values and how you approach them.

The Value of THEM

Everyone has a value. And with that I mean, when they go into a meeting, they will also have core values and goals just like you that may or may not align with yours. If your boss is set on trash talking about a fellow employee, then you must think about the reasons behind their goal. Maybe they don't like that person and want to fire them. Maybe they are threatened by some of that person's behavior or by the person themself. They are afraid to lose face as others may have noticed certain insecurities. Maybe that person is a bad employee. This is where your knowledge of them becomes invaluable. Really think about their background, their circumstances, their goals, their past behaviors (patterns), and what they want to gain in life (and from that meeting). You can use that knowledge to then steer to outcomes that are fair. If that person that your boss wants to trash is a bad performer/coworker, then you do not have to be mean or unfair. You can give facts and observations, you can voice concerns, and you can offer insights if you can think of a way to better that person and the situation. If your boss is threatened by that person, you can offer a different perspective, or at minimum, continue to stick to the facts, confirming that you have not observed any concerns. Offering a different perspective can achieve a lot, especially if your boss has a one-track mind or approach, and they often fail at reading people correctly. Always avoid addressing weaknesses directly and direct your insights to the person under scrutiny. Don't say, "I can't believe you can't see how sensitive Susan (sorry, Susan) is about XYZ." Start with, "I've noticed that Susan is sensitive when it comes to XYZ [because in her past, she has experienced ABC], which makes her very defensive when approached without notice." But base any feedback on facts and do not divulge secrets sure to do more damage. You are deflecting from your boss to a noted behavior, and maybe this will offer insight into that behavior for a better general understanding of that person (Susan). Susan has a value. To your boss and to you. Be fair in your assessment, stick to facts or personal experiences (observations), and acknowledge that Susan is a human being that happens to not have a voice in that moment.

Here's another value to consider about them. Think about what they can offer you or what you seek to obtain from them. Mentorship, a promotion, more money, friendship, support, freedom, commitment, joy, etc. Then consider what they had to go through or experience in order to get to their position. How did they gain that value that you now want? Can you appreciate their own struggles and accomplishments? Yes, you may like/dislike them, respect them, even loathe them. That's one part. But do you know their whole unabridged story? Value that they have values. You are not the only one with goals and emotions. Remember when I described one of my coworker's appearance and corresponding behavior? Despite his leadership shortcomings, he was a good person with good values, and he meant no harm. You must approach all your opponents with the same understanding to be/remain fair and objective.

The Value of Learning and Observing

The previous chapters (and this one) are stepping stones with one purpose: awareness of yourself, others, environments, goals, values, triggers—all with intent for continuous improvement. It's hard for me to describe, but the more you can learn and observe, and then see a value for everyone involved, the easier it will be for you to have meaningful and predefined interactions that will empower you and others.

Hopefully, in the last chapter, I will be able to connect the dots better. Beforehand, let me try to give you a little glimpse using the horse again. Once I understood that the horse was a mirror of my behavior, I also understood that I had the power to influence the horse and hence change the direction of my rides. That was a small breakthrough in my mind: I have the power to impact the outcome of the horse's reaction. (Versus me *reacting* to the horse, which was simply reacting to me in the downward spiral of miscommunication.)

I gave you glimpses of my adjustments in the previous chapter. First, I took lessons, and I learned the basics with little awareness and with a very narrow approach and mindset. The next step was a new trainer with a different approach that included the horse (my opponent) as part of my equation, including the environment. There came the realization that I wasn't listening to the horse and the horse wasn't listening to me (while the horse was reading me clearly and reacting to me), which made me pay attention to visual signals and observe reactions (also with the help of my trainer). Based on my expanded awareness, I was able to change my approach and my reactions, ultimately turning into the person empowering action—with the horse reacting with expected purpose. Finally, I had shifted into DRIVE. My interactions became fair, and I was able to value them for that fairness. What I put in, I got out. If I didn't pay attention to a trigger or a reaction, then I was less successful at my task. I kept learning and observing. At least I was driving now.

The Value of Valuing

I'll ask again: What is value? Value is everything all the time. Assigning value will help keep your actions and intentions fair.

There is value in everything and everyone. See the beauty, the effort, the impact, the importance, the danger, the risk, the potential, the love, the unknown, the hardship, the brilliance. Look at your world with a new appreciation of what it took to get there. Consider that other people have struggled, paid their dues, are great at something, can offer a new viewpoint or opportunity. Can you see? Can you grasp the concept that we are faced with values all the time?

REFLECTIONS & EXERCISES

VALUES are motivators. It is vital that you become aware of your own values and the values of your opponents. Every interaction serves to protect or promote those values.

Based on what you know about yourself (combination of experiences, observations, learnings, information, actions, beliefs, behaviors), can you determine what motivates/drives YOU?

I've shared my values in this chapter already. I found mine by looking at big past decisions to show me what was important to me in life. For example, if I had quit a job, then the reasons behind that decision were good indicators of what was important to me at that time. You, too, can use your past decisions to validate if you were protecting a certain value or pursuing another. Think of a major decision you have made. What was the driver behind that decision? Keep asking why until you reach your core values.

Alternatively, if someone ticks you off by pushing your buttons, determine why that is. What characteristic or core value is being attacked when someone gets under your skin?

How about your opponent? Based on the previous exercises (combination of experiences, observations, learnings, information, actions, beliefs, behaviors), can you determine what motivates/drives THEM?

Using my example, Napoleon, I arrived at my conclusions about his values easily because he was obvious in his behaviors and actions. You can review the previous write-up about him (the bold terms in the LEARN chapter exercises), to conclude:

Money (Greed): I would put that at the very top of his core values, and it was the motivator behind all his decisions. Not just to compensate for his physical size—since money builds a good buffer around insecurities—but also because he loved spending it to pursue fun activities, like traveling, eating at fancy restaurants, trying new trinkets, experiencing worldly adventures; that's what he wanted to do—not spreadsheets, budgets, managing, or strategizing. The business allowed him his freedom, so his focus was on driving his employees to give more for less so that he could spend more. Putting down people with negative comments and criticism enabled him to justify no raises or bonuses, even when the company performed extremely well. He also didn't want to share the profits or lower his expenses because he already had to "give his hard-earned money away to sisters who didn't contribute."

Authority (Acceptance/Recognition): It's never easy when the second generation takes over a business. Napoleon's father was a legend—he was also much shorter than Napoleon—and to me, they were completely different in character. Napoleon's dad was quiet, unassuming, proud of people, humble, focused, hardworking, secure in himself, and committed to the business. I didn't see any of that in Napoleon. Napoleon surely must have tried to live up to his father's reputation, but I don't think he ever felt that he measured up. His sisters confirmed it with their constant criticism. Additionally, it's hard to gain respect from employees who have been loyal to the father and who now must embrace nepotism. While it's a natural succession in privately held companies, Napoleon's employees always saw him as having been placed in a made nest without having to do any actual work. And unless you put in that work to gain the respect of your employees, then you will also never measure up to them. This was a struggle for Napoleon. For him to retain his authority, he had to tear down everyone else's.

Furthermore, because of his size, it appeared that he had the innate need to constantly prove something to everyone. That made any interaction difficult, knowing that he was extremely sensitive to all his shortcomings. This, combined with his sisters questioning his authority and capability, made being a woman in leadership in his company very challenging. Everything I did or said fell under intense scrutiny, was judged harsher, and had more severe and public consequences. It's also a bit ironic that he sought recognition and acceptance himself while denying the same to everyone else. Mind you though, he made a conscious effort to shake hands with his employees because he had heard that they felt more included and valued if he did so. He made everyone feel acknowledged, yet he wasted no time to criticize to put them in their place at the same token.

Power (Control): It's last on the value list because, in a way, he always had the power as a private business owner.

He didn't have to worry about being outvoted or outed. The threat of being fired was always there for those who disagreed with him, especially since he loved saying how everyone was replaceable. Nonetheless, power was important to him; but make no mistake about it, he only had it because he had money. He was aware of that circumstance, and he hated that he could not yield it without it.

There were also good values (**Parental Responsibility**): He cared for his children deeply, and he enabled them to pursue what they loved. If you're wondering, the company never made it to its third-generation owners. Napoleon sold out to a large conglomerate once the financials were in a good place to ensure the best price. It was most likely a win-win. He could pursue his travels and fun activities while the employees gained a different management structure where decisions were based on performance. Granted, with money as its core value. Some things never change.

He could be generous (**Entitled Generosity**): I was the recipient of a brand-name washer and dryer. They were his old units imported from Germany decades earlier that had been collecting dust in the company's warehouse for years since he did not want to gift them at that time. Still, he remembered that I had bugged him about them taking up space at work. When I resigned after fourteen years, I received gifts that were extremely amazing. It also wasn't uncommon for him to hold a company party at his house where he would cook for everyone (while the company was still small), or he would pick an artsy restaurant when we were bigger.

Privately, he was very easy to talk to. He was interested in everything, and of course, he had tons of stories to tell about his travels. He did not make you feel unworthy in private settings.

I know he got divorced from his first wife because he realized that life was too short to be unhappy. Now you may not see this as a positive, but I applaud anyone who pursues happiness and is honest about it. I can't help but admire people who know what they want in life and go after it. He was one of them.

He didn't mean to be mean. He had simply lost touch with his beginnings and the people who made them possible. As people progress on the corporate ladder, it is easy to forget the bottom. His reaction to women was automatic, and I bet, to this day, he remains oblivious to that. He simply failed at learning more about himself and others because life was catering to him most of the time. You don't need to try to appease when you're the boss. He grew up knowing that he would be the owner of a business, and he never had to pay much attention to his actions or his surroundings.

Based on my example, can you draw conclusions about your opponent's values? Pick the top three or four, include a positive value as well, and explain how you arrived at your conclusions. Can you validate them based on their behaviors, looks, patterns, etc.? You must not make assumptions. There will be something in your past and in the huge data dump of them in your brain that will support your findings (meaning, your brain has recorded a lot of data on them over time that will help you determine their values).

In our final exercise for this chapter, I want you to acknowledge the EMOTIONS. Emotions are normal and healthy, and we will make use of them. Emotions are our friends!

Time to relive the same interaction from the previous chapter. This time, let your emotions come up and connect them to an action. Could be tied to your action, your reaction, or their action or reaction. Of course, this exercise will be a lot easier if you have done the previous ones in writing. (It's never too late to start.)

Focus on the emotion in the moment. For example, when he leaned in to shake your hand with his sweaty hands and bad breath, were you disgusted, afraid, mad, intimidated? Can you figure out why you had those feelings? Relive the feeling with honesty. These feelings can feel uncomfortable. You may try to suppress them. Don't. Let them surface. If recalling something makes you want to cry, then cry. If you get mad, run five miles. If you feel happiness, enjoy. Dance for a minute, celebrate.

Was there something specific in an action that triggered a noticeable reaction? What was it? A gesture, a word, a touch? There had to be something there that pushed an emotion upward.

Here's another approach if you can't quite succeed: What emotions do you feel when you remember any uncomfortable situation? Think about what truly made you squeamish. The action or your feeling to it? You are looking for a trigger or a pattern of consistent behavior to an emotion.

Granted, you may not see a trigger or pattern yet. You may have to repeat the interaction exercise or relive others before an emotion tied to a repeat behavior becomes apparent. I bet when feelings involve shame or guilt, there's a definite trigger you must explore. Chances are those feelings could be based on something that happened in your past, way back when. Don't lie to yourself. Nobody's watching; you're safe, dig for it. There could be trauma you've been trying to hide because you don't want to acknowledge it. You will never own it if you don't own it. It will own you if you can't release it. First step is acknowledgment.

Finally, think about your opponent's emotions. Did you observe any emotions? If so, can you tie them to an action? Did their facial expressions, body language, tone of voice, verbal phrases, movement, etc. give any indication about how they felt in any moment during your encounter? Also think about the values that each of you were protecting or pursuing in this interaction. Can you see how some of the actions were influenced by the values?

Take a break. We can continue whenever you're ready for more. Be proud of your progress. The simple act of reading this book has already resulted in more awareness without you even trying. You are already seeing so much more.

Time to put this into empowerment.

CHAPTER 4: EMPOWER

Empower to empower.
That's the ultimate goal.
But first, let's empower you.

Learning, observing, and valuing will allow you to look at people, places, items, environments, circumstances, and the associated interactions with new meaning and control. I say "control" because it will feel like you have more control as you will be able to anticipate emotions/triggers/reactions/behaviors, which in turn will help you steer interactions to where you want them to go. Or at minimum, you will protect your values. And each interaction will teach you something new, which will help you with all future interactions. Use one to build on the next. Wash, rinse, repeat.

None of this will happen overnight. You must continuously apply learn, observe, and value before you can be empowered with more intent, purpose, and control. In the beginning, you will miss a lot. That's totally normal. However, you will also notice a lot more than you have before. While I am a lot better at my interactions now, it doesn't mean that I master all of them. But I learn from each. And simply the knowledge of being more aware each time gives me strength and encouragement.

Don't be disappointed or discouraged. There never is one quick fix. Those interpersonal challenges also did not pop up overnight. It took time, experiences, and a pattern of behavior to establish them. Never look at impact as one major occurrence or as the instant cure-all to all your interpersonal struggles. L.O.V.E. is a process, and what you have learned—everything up to now and everything going forward—will lead toward an empowered you.

It will feel so insignificant at first. You may even think that there is no impact. You'd be wrong. Impact means to have affect. Everyone and everything affect someone or something all the time. You've been on the receiving end of the wrong side of that stick. You are impacted by others in their pursuit of their goals. What you want is the other end: the one where you affect others to drive the right kind of impact for your benefit.

You either let it happen, or you make it happen.

"Karma is a bitch." How often do we say that, and then we wait for karma to arrive? Karma can take its sweet time, and as you wait, you undoubtedly wonder why you feel like such a doormat in some interactions while your opponent reaps all the benefits. Why are they successful? Were they born with the awareness that makes them intuitively impacters versus impactees? I dare say no.

Whether your toughest opponent is male or female, they most likely share these traits: They are clear on what they want out of life, and they know what it takes to get to their end goal because they have put a lot of thought and planning into where they want to be. In addition, they may behave in a certain dominant way that has proven successful over decades. This behavior is associated with taught male gender traits, such as interrupting, speaking over or ignoring others as well as being authoritative, unapologetic, and unempathetic.

But there are different drivers for male and female opponents to explain that type of behavior. First, the males: As outlined in the LEARN chapter, boys encounter fewer social rules growing up, which teaches them that it is okay to interrupt or speak over others as potential leaders. To society, that behavior is assertiveness; whereas, when a girl does it, that behavior is viewed as inappropriate and rude. Inappropriate behavior does not change depending on gender, yet our society continually excuses bad male behavior, allowing boys to grow up confident in themselves, their egos, and their actions. As men, they can rely on a support system (patriarchy), and they generally have less risk or fear of losing their jobs going into confrontations or interactions than their female counterparts.

Second, the females: Some women simply have adopted male-designated behaviors. This includes showing less emotions, appearing less vulnerable, voicing less empathy while becoming louder in opinion, making harsher decisions, and buying into the corporate rhetoric. They have seen what it takes to be "successful," especially in corporate America, and they have decided to adopt this behavior as the easiest way up the corporate ladder. And while there's still a double standard for when women act like men, it has helped some women establish themselves as "part of the pack," resulting in their inclusion in the club. Even outside a corporate setting, women can use a more male approach to attack or defend their interests with less risk of retribution (since they appear to be tough and unyielding).

Reasonable people will never be opponents you fear or worry about because they, well, reason. They will be able to see both sides of the coin, and they will make every effort to hear and acknowledge you. Interactions with reasonable people will most likely end in fair outcomes.

Those, male or female, who come on very strong in their interactions to push only their agendas, have learned that a certain behavior gets them rewards because, well, not just because it has proven successful in the past but also because you have allowed it to happen. They are simply taking advantage of you yielding and relenting control. They have accepted taking from the weak and the vulnerable without giving their actions a second thought because that's what privilege affords them.

Do not be hard on yourself for allowing them to impact you. Women were meant to struggle at self-care, which would help them to become aware so that they could fight with more conviction for themselves. The hole—that we have to dig out of after birth to get to where we are (or want to go)—is a crater filled with responsibilities, expectations, and organized exclusion, courtesy of the patriarchy. That fact alone should give you the courage and determination to continue with L.O.V.E. Look how far you have come! Men aren't smarter, more aware, or better than women. When you look at how we've had to fight for everything, it is crystal clear that women are exceptional, resilient, and strong.

Understanding that we never had a level playing field should be all you need to acknowledge your false perception of what you have believed to be your internal weaknesses, keeping you from succeeding. Make peace with the uneven playing field and use your awareness to balance out this inequity. Success cannot be defined by one interaction alone, but each will get you closer.

For example, your goal could be to survive a performance review with a harsh superior who always belittles you. Your past reviews went horribly, and all you ever walked away with was an earful of false perceptions presented by your boss. You dread your next review and just want it to be over. Firstly, and obviously, that's a horrible approach. Surely you will live through that performance review. No matter what, you will be okay in the grand scheme of things. The planet will keep spinning. Rewire your thinking to look forward to trying out a new approach instead. This next review will be a learning opportunity for you and your opponent. The only way is up for you. However, you must prepare. Time is your friend. You cannot start the process the night before. Here's what you do: Take notes of your (recent) accomplishments, i.e., how you have helped a customer or coworker, how you finished a task in record time without errors, how reliable and dependable you are (you're never late, sick, etc.), how you mentor others, or how you jump in to help out where help is needed. Additionally, if you have made a mistake, note how you have addressed it, corrected it, grown from it. How you took charge of whatever happened, and you made it okay. Record dates, times, projects, customers, team members involved. Familiarize yourself with your notes and arguments as this will ensure that you will not ramble incoherently and emotionally. Presenting facts calmly and without emotions will give you integrity. In past interactions and when confronted with criticism, you probably had an emotional response because you had no data at that time to disprove them (and so you took things personally). There's nothing more frustrating than having a false perception find its way into a permanent record.

It is vital that anytime you have achieved something or have received praise, you make note of it to use in the representation of your facts when you come under attack. Bring the notes with you to keep you on track. That record of your accomplishments and your consistent work ethics will be hard to dismantle when you can show instances that prove your statements. Your rebuttals can start with, "It is interesting that you see it this way. Remember when we had the ABC situation? That was quite a difficult spot to be in, but I managed it in such a way that our company benefited hugely." Here it is important not to make it about feelings, so do not use, "I think, You think, I feel, I believe, You felt." A feeling bears no weight, because, well, it's a feeling and not a fact.

This way of presenting yourself will take some practice, and I encourage you to come up with your supporting statements ahead of time. You must create, learn, and recite them with confidence.

At the same time, you can also record observations (but they must be factual) of your supervisor that could set a pattern of ill behavior, such as unfair treatment that you can support with documentation. When that review goes sour, even based on presented facts, then you should be able to lean on the HR department for support and intervention. There's nothing wrong with insisting on HR being present (if they are not) during the review if you are concerned about objectivity. If HR fails you, then that will be a good indicator of your success in that company in general as its value is not on employees or fairness.

Don't forget to utilize other resources when trying to prepare. As mentioned in the LEARN chapter, you can ask others if they can offer examples of how you have helped them. Find out how they have dealt with this person. Observe their interactions with that person. What do they have in common? What do they talk about (when it's not about work)? If your supervisor is big into music, there's an opportunity to find out what genre they like, if they play an instrument, belong to a band, etc. Just the tiniest effort on your part to make small talk, to compliment them, or to inquire about their interests will give you better circumstances in the long run. People with big egos love to be admired and to be the center of attention. You can play to their vanity without having to put on a fake act. Look at your adversaries as people. People aren't innately bad. Get fodder to help drive your impact down the road.

Make use of learn, observe, and value. Deal with the discomfort of your fear, feelings, anxiety while acknowledging all that you know about them and yourself. Just prior to the meeting, review your notes to remind yourself of your awesomeness. Take five minutes ahead of time to relax, do some breathing exercises, look over your notes (again), go to the bathroom, or give yourself a pep talk. Don't forget to bring your notes to the meeting. Once there, notice your surroundings, the items in the room and their placement, your opponent's clothes, expressions, words, gestures. Find some similarities in items (music, football), and lead into the conversation by establishing synergies. Try to make a connection. You will notice so much, and it will give you strength. There's control in that awareness. If you get to a point where you do not have answers or a rebuttal, then state that you will have to get back to them when you have done your research. Pressure is one of those things people will use to make you rush into an answer that will most likely never benefit you. Take deep breaths and tell yourself to slow down. This will be easier when you have prepared your facts and answers.

When conversations turn ugly, such as when they escalate into major disagreements, you can also disarm your opponent with the following statements: "I can understand why you reached that conclusion," or, "I can see your point." This will definitely take the edge off as your opponent will not have expected this. It allows for a pause to restart the conversation professionally. It shows that you see common ground while not admitting to anything or agreeing with your opponent. After this reset, you must use caution to dismantle your opponent's misconception with facts and without accusations or emotional references. Consider that most people don't want things to escalate.

You may think they do, but it is stressful to be in tense situations for anyone, no matter how strong they think they are. It is so much easier to deal with conflict when everyone keeps their negative energy levels low. It is also important not to interrupt your opponent when you feel wrongly portrayed. Wait until the points have been made and then calmly address the accusations. If you are still super anxious, that's okay. With preparation, this review will be different from before. And even if you consider your review a failure, remind yourself how you measure that failure. If you noticed more, even in hindsight, you have already done better. That's failure redefined into success. You have improved, and that is what you are looking for. You'll do better next time. Identify that one thing that was your biggest hinderance and work on it. For example, if all your words came out wrong, then consider a few options: Read more. I'm not saying read more fantasy or romance, but maybe get some self-help books on conflict resolution. Join a book club where you can practice discussing different viewpoints. Take an improv or acting class, which will force you to think quickly on your feet in unknown situations. Toastmasters is a great organization that is all about helping you speak in front of people. You can hone any skill that you are currently lacking that could help you in your most difficult interactions. Simply be honest about what investment could give you the best return. Then LEARN. I promise that one by one, you will gain confidence and traction. Interactions aren't necessarily about winning. Interactions are about learning, cooperation, fairness, honesty, value, and influence (= impact longterm).

The Secret Ingredient

It's called manipulation. There will be those who will criticize me for telling you to manipulate others. I'm okay with that. Managing people is all about manipulation.

Nobody wants to admit it. But what is manipulation? Isn't everyone trying to achieve an agenda or a goal when interacting? Isn't the purpose of any meeting to get someone to agree on something or to make someone see your point of view? Especially the men in your life? This makes the word MANipulation super relevant and to the point. Why does manipulation have to be such a negative?

Synonyms for manipulation are "handling" and "management." Exactly. I tried to find the antonym for manipulation. Here's what popped up: abstain, unmoving, powerless. We don't want to do or be any of those, so I think manipulation puts us on the right track. Additionally, manipulation, just like influence, cannot be defined by unknown intent, and any dictionary that adds a negative connotation does so by reflecting a false narrative. Think about how manipulation is used in medical and industrial sectors in describing how something or someone is skillfully maneuvered or treated by something or someone. By practicing L.O.V.E., you will enhance your manipulation efficacy. Make peace with manipulation. Humans are manipulators.

Your manipulation will look like de-escalation, proactivity, preparedness, and willingness to work together. You will be steering and redirecting actions with purpose, grace, and clearheadedness to preserve the objective of the interaction. How will you do this? By using everything you know to help drive your interactions with purpose. And "everything" literally means everything. What you have learned and observed about yourself and them (history, experiences, patterns, triggers, behaviors, appearances, events, timing, locations, circumstances, temperature, visuals, body language). The goals and objectives that are at the forefront for each participant, alongside the values that the opponent represents that you want to take advantage of. You anticipate different scenarios, and you can use every detail to help manage your opponent and the situation so it remains in the safe zone where there is no super escalation of emotions. Think of your encounters as a chess game where you have anticipated most of the moves.

It will be tiring and overwhelming as you try to apply your newfound powers. But the more you use your brain to make those connections about what it knows about you, them, the past, the values, the objectives, the location, the circumstance, then it will get easier and more intuitive. The more you become aware, the stronger you will feel your empowerment. I don't know how else to put this. All your knowledge is always available to you if you make the effort to utilize it with awareness.

Your new approach will blow your mind—because you used to be the oppressed, the one who could be controlled. Not anymore. If you do it well, your opponents will feel great about themselves while believing they still have power. Anytime your opponent can walk away with a positive feeling over a negative one, then that is a win-win, especially if you will continue to have to work with this person on a consistent basis. Disarm them without them knowing so that you can use each encounter as a building block for your next one. Little by little, you will be chipping away at that control that someone else has over you with impact that seems invisible at first. Consistency in your approach is important, as is learning something from each interaction that you can improve on for the next. Manipulation will be the karma you can impact.

However, commit to (and strive for) interactions that do not cause excessive harm to your opponent or yourself. As in, don't be evil. Be smart, aware, and remain integral to yourself and your values. This may sound surprising. You have looked at them as being evil, and you cannot imagine how you could ever be like them. Trust me, you will eventually see how it can be hard to remain true to your values as you grasp the concept of L.O.V.E.

More on that later.

Let's Take a Look

It's time to put my words into some visuals for you. I'm going to show you a few of my past interactions so that you can see some of the things that played into them. These interactions will seem boring and normal. Pay attention, though, there's a lot built into them disguised in that normalcy. I will start out by introducing two more characters in addition to Napoleon, whom you have met already. I will describe them, list their values, explain the larger objective, offer interaction examples, and then finish with my rundown on each.

The Downer

You know the type. The glass is always half empty, everyone is an idiot, same shit same day, same shit different day, different day same shit, different shit same day, life sucks, and then you die. Downers suck the positivity right out of you. They are a malignant cancer, and they will infect everyone and everything in their path.

My Downer was a service technician, German, and he worked for Napoleon, just like me. He liked to drink and party in his downtime. His hands shook all the time. His clothes were on the casual side, his dark hair was curly, thinning, and slowly receding. His lips were permanently downturned, hiding large teeth and an overbite. When he spoke, it was never about expressing pleasantries or kindness. He was constantly complaining about something or someone. He loved comparing America to Germany, and not once could America measure up.

He was single, of course. No woman was ever good enough. She had too many flaws, wore too much makeup or not enough makeup, spoke too loudly or too softly, or was too dumb (never too intelligent, though, because she didn't exist).

His work ethic sucked. He didn't do follow-ups or customer service (they were all idiots), and he never took ownership of his area of assigned expertise. He always had excuses and blamed others. When confronted about a nonperformance or an agreed-upon task that didn't get completed, he would often lie about his schedule or make up ridiculous reasons for why things didn't get done. He loved stating that he had no boss. He wasn't used to women standing up to him, and he would get upset easily when provoked with facts. He often slammed doors, and he would sulk for days after confrontations.

The Downer Expanded

He had worked for a mobility company in Germany before joining the company. He was into fast motorcycles and built a custom bike all by himself. He purchased a house in the States, even though—obviously—America sucked, and his work visa was tied to his employment, meaning that he would have to leave the country if he lost his job. Nonetheless, he valued his house as a place that felt like home.

He portrayed an outward and inward image of machoism. His look was one of toughness: long unkempt hair, five-o-clock shadow, jeans, dark T-shirt, black leather motorcycle jacket, and black shoes. Yet, it wasn't his appearance that made him unattractive, it was his behavior and demeanor. Everything about him was negative: his mouth tight, his eyes squinty and restless, his walk confrontational, his index finger quick to find its way in front of your face—his entire aura was grim.

He had always fallen under the radar and under someone's protection at work. He could deflect when confronted, knowing his job was safe. He also felt that he had an *in* with Napoleon, seeing that they were from the same region in Germany, and both liked to make rude comments about women or pick on the weak and vulnerable. He would suck up to Napoleon, trying to please him (just not with work). His visa depended on him, so he ensured to stay on Napoleon's good side.

Takeaways: He never saw himself as a problem because it was always other people's faults. Interacting with someone who is oblivious to their flaws, and therefore unwilling to learn and cooperate, can be extremely frustrating. He was single because he feared a meaningful relationship that would force him to evaluate himself in it and/or partake in the actual relationship. Relationships take work, and it was clearly something he wanted to avoid on an emotional level. He protected himself from feelings that would have included love and empathy for another being due to fear of having to show such feelings and appearing weak (human). His outer shell was extremely thick, even impenetrable, because he didn't want to face any emotions. I can assume that there had to have been some trauma in his life for him wanting to be so shut off from any feelings. He preferred loneliness over fear of getting hurt. When people are instantly aggressive or defensive in their behavior, then my assumption is that this is just their defense mechanism kicking in. I feel sorry for people on the defensive. It must be so draining trying to keep everyone out. I see Downer as a child who has never been taught about unconditional love, and he was probably never told that he was good enough for anything.

Downer's Values:
- Laziness/Indolence
- Friends with benefits
- Self-protection (emotional)/Preservation

- A place to call home
- Independence

The Narcissist

Narcissists surely don't lack confidence, arrogance, or a sense of entitlement. My Narcissist came to work for Napoleon as a newbie to our industry. He was hired as a VP, even though the size of our company did not warrant excessive layering of executive titles. Yet he insisted. He had worked at some large companies previously, and it became clear quickly that he expected to do very little actual work. He was disappointed that he had no secretary who could take care of the minutiae of travel schedules, coffee, and reports. He was from Irish descent, which he was very proud of. He had almost black, somewhat wavy hair, and he dressed businesslike, suits on big days, business casual on most days (khakis, polo shirt). He carried his large frame on small feet like he had a stick up his behind, a belly protruded from his center, and he thought his Irish charm worked on everyone.

He had confidence when faced with tough customer discussions as he could argue extremely well in the sales arena. He drew the line and stood firm on the company's objectives and fought some hard battles with customers during price negotiations. He could argue and make his points with Napoleon without an instant rebuttal.

He loved power and authority, and he used his large and loud presence to intimidate. When making decisions, they were made in the interest of his status quo and/or monetary benefits before considering those for the company or the team. "All for one, but not one for all" was his motto.

The Narcissist Expanded

He had lost his big job and salary, alongside the trophy wife, the McMansion, the fancy car, and other entitlements in the 2008 economy crash, and even years later, he had not recovered financially or emotionally, nor had he lost any of his arrogance. He said it humbled him, but his actions showed otherwise.

He had a huge appreciation for pretty women who didn't give him any contradictions. He thought of himself as quite the ham with his piercing blue eyes, definitely his best physical feature.

He fell in love with a troubled woman and provided her with stability and support. They got married years later.

He loved invading people's personal space, especially hovering over their shoulders at their computers where escape was impossible. He reminded the employees, customers, and vendors of his importance. Nothing seemed enough. He wanted more respect, power, authority, money, admiration, benefits, favors. When he wasn't traveling, he wandered into the office at his leisure, and he would also run long errands or leave early. He didn't include anyone in his plans, and when he did, it was only to give as much information as he needed for them to cater to him.

He admitted that he didn't like working for such a small company. The hands-on work was beneath him. He liked to reminisce about his past where his salary and support staff were more adequate.

He thought of himself as a patriot, and he often stated how the Germans were intentionally sabotaging him when he didn't like their decisions.

Takeaways: He felt more entitled to everything because he used to have it, he earned it, or it was given to him. He had never worked for a small organization, and he could not understand the fact that there weren't enough people to delegate work to. He simply remained stuck in the past. He longed for the glory days, and that desire would remain his top priority. Because he was entitled, everything revolved around him. His main goal in life was money, and he would use anyone and anything to get his hands on more.

He was not afraid to share his opinions with Napoleon as he felt secure in his title, job, and capabilities.

The woman he loved was very compliant, submissive, and unsure of herself. She was an easy subject to control. I'm not saying he did not love her. Nonetheless, she was a woman that would not give him any troubles or question his authority.

He had several children and was very committed to them. He loved them openly, supported them, and he was proud of them equally. He extended those values to his girlfriend the minute they became an item (he was long divorced by then).

Narcissist's Values:
- Money (Greed)
- Validation/Authority/Respect
- Control/Power
- Family
- Love of Country

Can you visualize them?

The Challenge & the Objective

I want to dive into what I was trying to achieve as operations manager at Napoleon's company. Downer and I had come to work for the American subsidiary at about the same time. My start had been as an office manager, but after eight years, I was promoted to operations manager when my former boss (and mentor) quit. Downer in the meantime had had a cushy time and job. While our company made self-adhesive labels for the automotive industry (product identifiers for tracking parts being assembled in a vehicle), his job was to work with the German HQ on U.S. equipment quotes, and once that equipment was sold, he was the service technician for maintenance and troubleshooting. There were, however, not enough sales throughout the years to keep Downer busy full-time. He didn't like sales or calling people, and being allocated to the service department allowed him to hide in his office for the most part. He had no one to motivate or guide him, and the absence of accountability and leadership was his reward for his indolence. It was a bad combination.

As you may imagine, his negativity and laziness impacted everyone at work. The employees hated him, he hated them, and whatever he worked on had a quality or intelligence level that left much to be desired, which also affected people down the line who had to deal with his limitations. One good employee quit because he did not want to be around Downer. Customers despised him because he was rude and unprofessional; he didn't return their calls, and he belittled them.

Since we were a small company, HR functions fell into my area of responsibility. (Companies with less than fifteen employees often do not have or need a full-time person to manage personnel matters. Additionally, having HR often acknowledges the need for action and translates to having to spend more money, two things most owners of small businesses want to avoid.) Effectively, our company was left to its own devices to deal with employee problems. I had done my best to work with my employees when it came to Downer, but it was more about damage control, seeing that I was unable to fire Downer myself.

Downer, in simple terms, was a liability to the company. I knew that we had to get rid of him. It was the right decision to be made for the business and the employees (and customers). Morale had been badly impacted. Downer's mood had spread throughout like a cancer and demoralized—even sabotaged—the entire team. What added to the frustration was that management (me included) didn't do anything about it. I tried but hadn't been successful in eliminating the problem.

Let's start with Napoleon. The below is a typical conversation about Downer. Mind you, after years of voicing my concerns.

The Napoleon (TN) Interaction

Napoleon arrives at work on his motorcycle. Having heard the bike, I make a point to greet him as he enters the building with his cell phone in hand and a backpack slung around his shoulder. I haven't seen him in months but was aware that he was in the country for a few days. I knew that he would make an appearance at work today.

He sees me approaching but doesn't acknowledge me in any way. He seems in a rush, pretending to look at his phone. I know he doesn't like it when interactions are not on his terms. Nobody likes to be assaulted the minute they arrive somewhere without getting settled first. It had been necessary though. Napoleon liked to get in and out (of the office), and I knew that he would slip through my fingers if I didn't get him to commit at the earliest opportunity to meet before he left. I didn't have access to his travel plans or schedules, so it was always hard to figure out the best meeting approach with him. Napoleon was more into vendor or customer interactions, and if I would have asked him ahead of time, he may have not come to the office at all. In his defense, me seeking him out meant that I wanted to talk about unpleasantries. I never had to involve him otherwise (for help or feedback).

I try to lighten his apprehension by speaking in my happy voice.

Me: "Welcome back!"

He looks up. I give him a big smile. He returns one, but it is quick and looks forced.

TN: "All good here?"

He doesn't wait for an answer and keeps walking past me toward his yellow office, making the point that he's got things to do (other than dealing with me). I follow. I notice how he did not shake my hand this time. It's because he doesn't appreciate being cornered. I get it.

Me: "Of course, but I was hoping to meet with you today."

I try to keep up with him as he hurries to his office. I will not be denied.

TN: "I have a call in a minute. And I can't stay long. You'll have to be quick."

Short sentences imply that he has no time. He's busy unpacking, looks everywhere else but my face as he places and shuffles items around on his desk. Avoidance.

Me: "I didn't mean to rush. Just want to make sure I catch you before you leave today."

I explain my early presence to take the edge off. I definitely would not want to talk to him now. He's flustered, and I know my chances of a decent interaction are already abysmal without his current agitated state. I stand up straight as I speak to him and am firm in my eye contact (when I finally get it), and I give determination to my voice to show that this is important enough for more time. I continue.

Me: "Do you want to meet after your call?"

I phrase the question to make him feel empowered (his choice).

He nods. His facial expression softens. He's relieved he's bought himself some time.

TN: "Later, for a few minutes, yes. For now, I'm going to get a coffee before my call starts."

He's not happy about our upcoming meeting, and he is trying to limit his exposure by pre-announcing a limited amount of his available time (a few minutes) when we do meet. It also says that he does not see the importance. He grabs his coffee mug from his desk and walks by me. He doesn't offer a time or timeframe for our meeting. Leaves me hanging.

I holler after him.

Me: "Thanks, just let me know when you're ready for me."

It is important that I verbalize his agreement to meet. The intent is to guilt him into remembering his commitment, but also, to let him know that I expect him to find me when he's ready.

He gives me a thumbs-up without turning around.

Hours go by. I keep checking on him by walking past his office every now and then. Napoleon has his door shut; I don't hear him or movement for most of my passes. I fear that he will leave without meeting with me. The door opens eventually, and since he's not in his office the next time I come by, I search and find him in the kitchen, putting his dirty coffee cup in the sink.

Me: "All done with your call? Is now a good time to meet?"

I stand in the doorframe, blocking an escape. He looks at me, noticing how I'm in his way. There's a slight frown on his lips for a split second. He doesn't like the situation.

TN: "I need to leave. I'm about to pack up my things."

His strategy is to either move the meeting to another day or to fluster me enough so he can rush me through it. He opts for the latter. His shoulders drop.

TN: "We can talk while I pack. Okay?"

The drop in his shoulders is an indication to me that he is shedding some of his defensiveness toward me. Or that he remembered his earlier promise.

I let him pass and follow him down the hall to his yellow office. He goes behind his desk and starts loading things into his backpack.

TN: "So what is it?"

He says it impatiently, letting me know that he anticipates bad news from me. Unfortunately, I won't be able to loosen him up more by making small talk about something that interests him. Internally, I'm anxious. He has forced my hand. But I had forced his as well. I remain as neutral as I can in my voice as I cut to the chase.

Me: "We need to talk about Downer."

He stops instantly. Looks at me with squinty eyes. I just triggered him. We've been down this road before, and I expected his lack of enthusiasm. I purposely chose the phrase "we" need to talk versus "I" to deflect attention away from me. Internally, I brace myself for the attacks that are sure to come.

TN: "What about him?"

He sounds exasperated.

I smile, raise my hands up—palms out toward him—defensively. I let him know that he's not very approachable. However, he could also view this as an apology.

Me: "I know it's a bit of a sore subject, but he's really impacting everyone's performance. John put in his notice last week because he said he's had enough abuse by Downer. The team's morale is at an all-time low."

I take myself out of the equation by avoiding any references to how I feel about Downer or how I think he's performing. By phrasing my concern in a neutral manner, it makes me look less vindictive to Napoleon. I position myself in the doorframe, hoping to keep him in the office for our conversation. Standing also offers me a slight height advantage over him; it makes me feel stronger while serving as a reminder to him that he's not as large as he thinks he is.

He gives me a questioning glare and then smirks.

TN: "I didn't get that feeling when I was out there on the floor. Everyone seems fine."

He is trying to deflate the severity of Downer's impact on the team. His chin tilts forward a tiny bit in defiance. Challenging me. I don't respond right away. Napoleon's statement wasn't an invitation to discuss the matter. Nonetheless, he expects me to contradict his statement. And I could offend him by calling him out on not being there consistently enough to have a good read on the team. But I avoid it and deflect myself (by ignoring his statement).

Me: "It's not just morale. Our customers are complaining that he's not returning calls, sending quotes, or following up on service requests."

Again, I make no reference to myself. I keep to facts. Theoretically, as a business owner, he should care about customers and business that he may miss out on. Customers pay the bills and allow him to pursue his fun activities. He rubs his chin. He hadn't anticipated my response. He's quiet for a few seconds.

TN: "I haven't heard anything negative from our customers or employees."

While he phrased this smartly (he probably hadn't heard from U.S. customers or other employees because he had not been the point of contact for either based on his constant absence), he should be aware of the ongoing issues with Downer. This is where it will get tricky since I now must call him out.

Me: "Well, you weren't directly involved, but I have copied you on email correspondence that outlines some of the recent concerns with Downer. Narcissist has gotten several calls complaining about Downer's lack of cooperation. It is impacting him as well."

He probably hasn't read any of my emails because they tend to be detailed and specific. Too long for his short attention span on a subject he doesn't want to deal with. I brought Narcissist into the equation to show that I'm not the only employee with concerns.

He gets defensive, his face looks slightly flushed. He raises his voice.

TN: "Do you know how many emails I get? I can't read them all. Especially when there are multiple attachments and references. You are overreacting. Nobody in Germany shares your opinion. I think you're trying to make a big deal out of nothing."

He's not just deflecting, he's also attacking. He mentions other people to prove that he's not the only one who thinks I'm wrong (just like I had done with Narcissist). I won't dispute him because it will not add anything of value. I can tell he's working on putting me in my place. I am aware of what he's doing, so I don't give into my trigger (emotion). I hook my thumbs on my belt loops and drop my shoulders. I'm showing him how unaffected I am by him. It gives me strength to know that I can keep my composure. I ignore his statement and attack the people (and him indirectly) who don't see Downer as a concern.

Me: "That's because they are too far removed from him. They don't know what he is or isn't doing. There is no accountability."

Another trigger for him as he considers any criticism toward Germany an attack on him.

He gives off an appalled huff.

TN: "Of course there is accountability. He reports to Sven, he talks to me, and he's got Narcissist. You aren't privy to those conversations and don't see what's going on. Why are you questioning the chain of command?"

He does have a point that the equipment portion and service are, in fact, not my areas of responsibility. I know as well as him that I have overstepped. He tries to convince me that everything is under control.

I ignore his question and instead offer a suggestion.

Calm Me: "He needs more direction, more hand-holding. He's a loose cannon. He is hurting the business."

Theoretically, this could be an olive branch: a step toward reconciliation to agree that there could be some improvements to the Downer situation.

Napoleon puts his hand on his hip, stretches his frame upward in an attempt to make himself taller. Takes a long breath in. Considers the olive branch for a second.

TN: "You just don't like him."

He says it with satisfaction and stares at me. I imagine him smiling on the inside. He just made it personal. It's hard to argue against such an accusation. A trigger for me as I take pride in my fairness as a leader. I'm aware of this trigger (not my first rodeo with him), and I don't acknowledge his perception of my personal feelings for Downer. It is important for me to remain factual and unemotional. I'm fuming internally, but I succeed at keeping my voice even. It shows that he didn't get to me.

Me: "Liking him or not has nothing to do with his work performance. He's killing our morale, he's making customers mad, and we could be selling a lot more on the equipment side if we had a person in that position who is more customer service oriented."

I try to remind him what he's missing (more sales). At the same time, there is no reason for me to hold back since he made it personal. When he does that, he considers a conversation over. However, it is important for me not to walk away first. Me sticking to my guns is letting him know that I cannot be intimidated. Internally, he is struggling. It's in his microexpressions as I speak to him. I can see his eyeballs move left to right as if in a panic, and his breathing has sped up.

He finally laughs, but it comes out like he was trying to spit. Waves his hand in a dismissive way. It's a signal that he wishes for me to disappear.

TN: "It's always the same with you and Downer. I'm tired of hearing you bitch when he's none of your concern. That's so unprofessional. Why can't you get it in your head that Downer works for me, not you?"

No better way to shut someone up than by way of insult and deflection. He also said the B-word, a clear indicator that I had gotten to him, and he couldn't refrain himself from hurling an insult at me. I snicker internally at the irony over his inability to see himself acting unprofessionally. Sure, at this point I'm also mad, but I won't let it show or affect my behavior. For now, I'm simply waiting for him to end our meeting. I say nothing because there would be no value or point. He takes my silence for submission, and it strengthens him to continue his attack.

TN: "You know nothing about equipment sales or service. You want to get rid of Downer because it's personal to you. You've been out to get him for years."

He shakes his head and waves me off again.

Internally, I want to scream at him because it upsets me that he believes my reasons to be personal versus factual. But trying to defend myself will not accomplish anything. It would not make him change his opinion. I make my point one last time as calmly as I can. I can't quite hide the quiver in my voice because I'm frustrated, and there are many other choice words swirling around in my head. I hate hearing the quiver, but it is what it is. For me, it's important to say what must be said, even if my voice is shaky and he will pick up on my frustration.

Me: "I want to get rid of him because it's the right thing to do for the business."

I am not afraid to agree that my plan is to get Downer fired. That is, and should be, the best decision for the company and its employees. My job as the manager of that business is to work in the interest of the business (not the owner). I align myself with the business objective. I know, though, that anyone who claims to understand HIS business better than him is another trigger for him.

We glare at each other. He squints.

TN: "It is MY business, and as such, you don't have the slightest clue how to run it, especially when it comes to sales. You are sticking your nose where it does not belong. Downer does not work for you. He's not your concern. I don't want to hear you mention him again. End of discussion."

He flings his backpack on his shoulder. I remain quiet. I know it's best to keep my mouth shut at this point.

He smiles when he realizes that he has won.

TN: "Anything else?"

He says it challengingly, knowing that we're done and that I will let it go because the consequences could be severe if I didn't.

I shake my head while trying to calm my nerves and slow my breathing. I unclench my fists when I notice my nails digging into my palms. I exhale slowly and quietly as I back away from the door into the dark hallway, allowing him space to pass. I'm hoping the darkness will cover my tight lip and other microexpressions that I can't stop from appearing.

His face shows defiance, and he adjusts his backpack as a signal to me to retreat to my office. I don't though. I make a point to stick around. I force my facial features to relax, along with my shoulders, while hovering in the dark hallway. I want my appearance to say that I'm not too bothered. Forcing a smile, I respond.

Me: "Nope, all good."

I try to sound cheerful.

He passes me and walks toward the front door on short, quick legs.

Okay, let me get the gnome out of the penthouse. You may say that I had no success. That I failed at achieving anything of value. You are right and you are wrong. Obviously, I did not get Downer fired. But that also wasn't my objective for that particular meeting. After eight years of previous less-confrontative encounters with Napoleon when it came to Downer, I knew that I had no chance of success. My objective simply was to state the facts and to do the right thing for the business. It's not winning that defines your success. It's about what and who you represent during your interactions as well as picking up on the little nuances that used to go unnoticed.

His objective had been one of avoidance. He was unable to ignore me or to delay our meeting. How do you think he felt having to remain in a conflict situation? How he had to resort to insults to get his objective accomplished because he let his triggers get the better of him? How he had to fight dirty?

Never make your emotions or feelings the center point as they will shut down your observation skills. Shift your attention away from yourself and focus on your opponent as your observational mirror and lens. This is positive reinforcement in your new way of looking at things from another perspective. One that is not about your feelings but about what factually happened to the other person that you did not notice before because you were too focused on yourself (how you felt and how you failed). Readjust your viewpoint. What could you observe in his responses? Ask yourself, "Was it something that was said or done—or both?" There is a value (and an opportunity) in your opponent's trigger.

To Napoleon, I was a reminder that he had weaknesses, and I triggered him to be overwhelmed by his emotions because he could not deal with me effectively otherwise. Despite his criticism, I rose above it. I'm certain that some of our interactions made him furious. He didn't expect my behavior and my calmness. He felt powerless despite having all the power. That is because I presented valid facts and arguments. All he could resort to were words full of emotions and void of logic because deep down he knew that he had nothing to counter me with. Don't you feel a wee bit sorry for such a man? I, on the other hand, did not feel powerless in the above interaction despite knowing that I could never win. Make peace with that. You may have a Napoleon in your life who will always have the last word. In that case, your goal must be to uphold your values while not risking your job. The key is to acknowledge the ineffectiveness regarding your larger objective before going into the interaction and to focus on what you can impact, learn, and observe instead. Don't set yourself up to fail; instead, shift to what you can take away from this meeting that will empower you down the line. Redefine your success, not your failure.

My composure and preparedness were huge factors in establishing boundaries with Napoleon. Napoleon was taught that I stood my ground with logic and calmness, and it intimidated him as could be observed by his avoidance of me. What does it say when you know your opponent doesn't want to deal with you? I'd say that's powerful. Trying to have small talk with him in the office could be fun. Since he expected me to only approach him with issues that needed his authority, his body language displayed his insecurities anytime I walked up to him. I took pleasure in that.

However, let's not forget that I had a secure position high up in the company, which allowed me to experiment with how far I could push Napoleon. Some of you will not have that luxury and need to be more cautious with your opponent.

Did you notice references to a yellow office in my encounter with Napoleon? I always found the color to be unsettling for an office. It wasn't a comforting or comfortable location. It felt too aggressive, and I'm sure it didn't help with anyone's inner peace. Consider that little things—which you may have ignored previously—can and will impact behavior. As weird as it may sound. That's why it is so important to really see everything with value and influence. If a yellow office has an impact, so do you.

Regarding circumstance and environment, give some thought to how Napoleon bullied his employees the moment he entered the building. Going on the attack ensured little resistance in the long run. He trained his employees to feel less worthy with his criticism while pretending to show false appreciation by shaking their hands. That impact of his behavioral pattern set the tone for any interaction with his employees. In that specific environment, any employee would be acutely aware of their faults when facing Napoleon. I'm not saying it was consciously intentional by Napoleon. But for him, it was the easiest way to prevent confrontation, raises, and recognition, and it affirmed his behavior because people didn't know how to countermeasure him. It gave him an advantage over his employees who felt less confident from the get-go when interacting with him or even when near him. He ensured that the scales were tipped in his favor.

And then consider how I had approached Napoleon. I encroached on him the minute he stepped into the building. I was aware of that circumstance. Still, given my experiences and interaction history with Napoleon, combined with his quick retreats (escapes), I believed it to be my best foot forward.

I didn't hate Napoleon. Napoleon was a child of his circumstances, background, society, culture, and unwillingness to learn about himself and others. I understood his reasoning and behavior. I knew what to expect going into our interactions. I was aware of my limitations with Napoleon, and, nonetheless, I kept trying because it was the right thing to do. I believed I could get Downer fired while acknowledging that the current method wasn't working. Remember: When one approach isn't working, then we must consider other avenues to get us to our end goal. I struggled for eight years to find the right approach.

Until Narcissist came on board.

Narcissist was a man who loved money and power. I came to realize that Downer represented a major hurdle to Narcissist, keeping him from earning commission. I set out to use that to my advantage and to the benefit of the company and all employees. I simply had to make Narcissist aware of the obvious obstacle and keep reminding him of the unnecessary drag on his income potential. Additionally, I was certain that Napoleon—having the same motivation (MONEY) as Narcissist—would be more inclined to listen to Narcissist (over me) if I could get him recruited to the cause. Even though Narcissist was another challenging obstacle due to his obvious flaws, I saw him as a friendly enemy. This is what I meant earlier: you can pursue other avenues when you hit the wall with that ONE person. You can use others who may have more influence with your impossible opponent.

While Narcissist was a friendly enemy—I saw a value in maintaining a good relationship with him—Downer was more of a nuisance to me since I had to work twice as hard to get him to cooperate. He didn't bring a huge value to the company. I didn't worry about my encounters with him, but Downer, being aware of my disapproval, did pose a challenge because it put him into a defensive mood whenever I approached. I didn't avoid Downer, knowing that he was defensive. It wouldn't take much provocation or normal conversation for him to say something that, under normal circumstances, would have gotten him sent to the HR department (if it had existed). However, in our interactions, Downer had learned to be more careful in what he said, being aware of my agenda and my willingness to debate issues. For me, the hardest part about Downer was drawing out actual and factual details to use against him.

The Downer (D) Interaction

I pass by his office with some documents in hand, pretending that they need to go to the archive section in the warehouse (on the way to Downer's office). The trip was unnecessary, but I set up my approach to make it appear random and less threatening.

Me: "Oh . . . hey, Downer, sorry to interrupt, but seeing that service part on your desk made me wonder if you've gotten the information back yet from Germany for the Widget quote?"

I specifically mentioned the part on his desk as a good lead into my interaction with Downer. If I would have barged in with a direct "Any news on the quote?" then he would have been completely shut down to me from the get-go.

He sits behind his desk, looking at his monitor.

D: "No."

A typical one-word response, and he doesn't offer more. He does not turn to look at me. He ignores me on purpose.

Tries to get rid of me with his short answer (also because I assume he didn't follow up with Germany and that he doesn't want me to know).

Me: "Ah, bummer. You know the customer expects to have the quote today based on the last phone call with Sven. We have pushed them off for weeks."

I try to sound as disappointed as I can to see if I can get more out of him. I remain in the doorframe, focused on Downer, making it clear that I'm not going anywhere. He finally looks up at me.

D: "I know."

He smiles quickly, then looks back at the monitor. He offers nothing else, despite acknowledging that a quote was promised today. I need to know more about what he did or didn't do before I can share the news with Narcissist.

I smile myself and nod. I'm content to go on with the cat and mouse game.

Me: "When did you talk to them last?"

I ask a direct question that, theoretically, he should not be able to answer ambiguously.

He looks back at me. Shrugs. Stares at me with tight lips. He's trying to come up with a response that doesn't make him look bad since a simple yes or no answer will not suffice. His puzzled expression tells me that he didn't talk to anyone recently. He stays silent, crosses his arms. I know he won't respond.

Me: "Did you call them first thing this morning?"

I get more specific in the timeframe. At the latest, he should have placed a call that morning. I also know he hates these suggestive questions; he's aware that I'm insulting him because he knows that I don't think he's doing his job. But I need facts from him that I can then present to Narcissist, so I keep digging. He remains quiet, looks away for a few seconds before he answers.

D: "Nobody answered."

His arms are still crossed. His stare is challenging, and his chin points up. I'm certain he's just lied; him looking away before answering and the quickness of his words are clues. Plus, he was not clear in his reply. He didn't say who didn't answer (but then, nobody can answer when nobody was called). Nonetheless, I keep prodding to see how far he can take his lie.

Me: "Who did you call? Did you leave a message? I need to let Narcissist know something."

I'm using Narcissist's name to deflect attention away from me pushing him. I probably should not have asked two questions at once, seeing that he typically half answers one question at a time. However, firing multiple questions at him is also a tactic I like to use to push him into an involuntary answer.

D: "I called Sven. Left a voice mail."

His voice is weak; the insecurity confirms to me he didn't call or leave a voice mail at all, and he doesn't want to admit it. I'm not satisfied with his answer. I'm interested in a solution or indication of a plan.

Me: "Have you tried him again?"

He's clearly annoyed, his body and face tense. Dislikes me questioning his sense of duty. He sneers at me.

D: "NO. Why would I? I left a message. He'll get back to me when he can. No need to call again."

He's making it clear that he will not call again, especially with me in the room. He focuses back on the monitor, uncrossing his arms. He continues staring at the screen, hoping for me to get the hint and leave.

I know he's uncomfortable, and I keep at it because I need to present facts to Narcissist.

Me: "Let's call him now. Together. That customer is really hounding Narcissist for a quote. And we promised one today."

I'm sure he'll never go for it. He doesn't look at me. He has no answer. I know he needs to deflect so that I cannot blame him for not having a quote ready while finding out that he never placed any calls in the first place.

D: "Why bother, they all left already. It's wasted effort."
You can taste his words. Lemons on the palate.

He continues staring at the monitor, hoping I give up. We both know that the Germans have most likely left the office already, seeing that it is Friday, and they are six hours ahead of U.S. time. They never stuck around Friday afternoons.

I don't give up because it was his job to secure a quote by today. Keeping promises is very important to me, and the company's reputation is tied to our ability to do so. I offer a suggestion of what he should have done proactively, knowing it will annoy him.

Me: "Did you not send them a reminder yesterday to make sure that they could provide the information today so we can prepare the quote? They've been pushing us off for weeks now. The customer will go elsewhere if we cannot give them a quote today. Germany promised us the quote."

I appeal to his German pride. Germans are known to be reliable, and by not presenting us with a quote, they must be bad Germans. Additionally, I point out that this has been an ongoing issue and that we could lose a potential customer. He shifts in his chair, and I enjoy watching him squirm. Finally, he looks at me with determination.

D: "They don't work for me. I'll get it when they are ready."

He's thinking that this should end the conversation. I wasn't expecting him to show any pro-activity, but I'm not ready to leave yet. I keep at it.

Me: "It's been weeks since we requested help from Germany. It's your baby, really. You must push and hold them to deadlines, remind them, follow up. We can't sell if we don't quote."

Downer knows that I can't do anything about his nonperformance. I have made it no secret that I have been complaining, but he feels protected. Nonetheless, he's aware that he can't be completely rude to me.

I make no effort to leave. He is contemplating if he should respond; his eyes are moving slightly without focus. He finally realizes that he will not get rid of me unless he cooperates a bit. He softens his facial expression, smiles, then shrugs.

D: "What can I say, it's not up to me. I'm just the messenger, don't blame me for them not getting to our quote."

Deflecting blame. I pretend to buy into his niceness, nodding my head in agreement.

Me: "I hear ya. It can't be easy having to rely on the Germans to actually pull through on their promises sometimes."

I'm being facetious on purpose, and the pun is not well received. Downer's eyes blink rapidly, and I can see him take a quick breath. I continue before he can fire anything back, and I do so in a softer voice.

Me: "I'm just trying to find a way to calm down our customer. Is there any chance you could make a budgetary quote so that at least we have something to present? We must save face with our customer. We can always state that we can firm up the numbers next week, but this way, we are not out of the race."

I want to show him that we can try to keep our promises even when others don't see the importance.

D: "Nope."

He doesn't offer a reason with this short answer. Shakes his head left to right. It's just part of the game for him. I oblige. I don't mind putting in the effort.

Me: "Why not?"

I keep my voice even while retaining eye contact.

D: "This is a completely new system. I'm not guessing; that would be stupid."

I nod; it is a feasible explanation. He smiles, knowing that he's made a good point. It is like pulling teeth with him. I don't give up easily; I think I'm a pretty good dentist at this point.

Me: "Is there anything you can do to speed this process up? Or can I or Narcissist help? We can get Napoleon involved."

I go in the opposite direction, offering my help. He does not expect it, and he is now forced to make excuses so that he won't have to take me up on the offer. Additionally, I hit a nerve mentioning Napoleon. He knows it's a threat, and I'm name-dropping to get him to act. He does act (in a way that I expect). His voice is slightly raised and annoyed. He has had enough of my inquisition.

D: "Quit telling me how to do my job. Napoleon knows about the delay. They get the quote when we get it. It's not like they're going to go elsewhere. We're the only ones who can help them."

His assumptions are lazy (and false). He makes a point to say that Napoleon is in the loop (which he probably isn't).

I do not push for the truth. There's nothing to be gained by asking Napoleon on his supposed involvement. More likely, it would firm up his opinion of me as the nagging bitch out to get Downer. Nonetheless, I make a counterpoint to Downer, showing that he has not considered all possibilities.

Me: "We can never assume that there isn't another company. I'm sure we are not the only players in this market."

He rebuts instantly with false confidence.

D: "They won't buy elsewhere. Not when they already have two of our machines at other locations. Makes no sense."

He loves saying that things don't make sense, implying that if they don't make sense, then they're stupid.

There's nothing else to do or say (it wouldn't make sense). I have what I need. I sigh on purpose, then smile.

Me: "Anyways, will you keep me in the loop on this quote, please."

He sizes me up (looks me up and down), unsure how to take the sudden stop in my interrogation and my false niceness. But he's happy I'm retreating. He bares all teeth; it's a mock smile. He gives them out frequently when he acknowledges something that displeases him internally.

D: "Sure."

When interacting with a Downer, it is important not to give in to his attempts to ignore you (or to get rid of you) when you need information. Remember that his values are avoidance and lack of details. You must ask direct questions (one at a time) so that he cannot deflect or be ambiguous. This is where you must exercise patience. Your persistent presence will be felt, and it will make your opponent uncomfortable. Prepare your questions in your head before you approach him and think of all the excuses or deflections that he may throw your way. Key is not to give up, keep the pressure on him, and you will see the shift in comfort. It is the same principle as with Napoleon. Part of their win is to make you go away so that they have to deal with less of their emotional triggers. How's that for impact?

When working with a Downer, I recommend backing up some of your interactions in writing. It could be an email confirming something or asking to clarify a point that was deflected on earlier. Though from experience, I can tell you that Downers may not respond with emails for the very reason of not wanting a written account of their (in)actions. However, you can circumvent that by including other people in copy that should care about the clarity of something. You can always follow up with a "Just checking on this email I sent three days ago," if you keep getting ignored. And if that Downer then comes to you in person or calls, you can still follow up with another email that says, "Confirming our earlier conversation, we have decided to XYZ." It should never matter what others say about your written obsession and diligence in transparency, especially when it can clear your name later on. A paper trail can be your best friend. It works for employees, coworkers, bosses, and Downers. Your documentation can serve as the burden of proof while exposing your opponent's past behavioral patterns.

You may wonder why Narcissist did not stay on top of Downer for the quotes he was supposed to secure. Narcissist surely was more negatively impacted than me. Sales wasn't my territory, and I could have let it drop. But I volunteered to be the go-between, so to speak. Here's the deal: Narcissist did not like Downer, who exhibited a lot of bad German traits (arrogance, ignorance, superiority, brotherhood). Germans can be very stuck in their patterns and cultural viewpoints. Additionally, customer service is not their forte (not even in Germany). The German HQ often treated us like the red-headed stepchild, which can be common when it comes to German ownership in U.S. companies. Germany took care of German business first. It irked Narcissist that the Germans would snub Americans, especially the ones with big titles. He had a hard time making friends in Germany because of that. The American sales approach of fake niceness is not appreciated by most Germans. I, on the other hand, had allies in Germany who could help with information. Since I spoke German, Narcissist also rightly assumed that Downer would rather deal with me than him. Country before gender, I guess. I had value to all since they didn't want to deal with each other directly. Narcissist thought he was using me, and he saw me as an ally who could verify Downer's information. Additionally, I could motivate the troops in Germany by circumventing Downer at times. And Downer was glad when I helped push for answers with the German counterparts since he was lazy. However, he also expected me to be sympathetic to the hardworking Germans who had so much to do that they couldn't deal with the less important American market with smaller margins. I kept everyone at bay, and my involvement prevented many heated confrontations.

I was a willing participant because I had my own agenda.

The Narcissist (N) Interaction

After my visit to Downer, I head over to see Narcissist to inform him of the latest Downer letdown. He's in his office, which happens to be gray in color. Gray is a great color for interactions as it does not provoke a visual distraction while, at the same time, subduing the energy that Narcissist could draw from if he would have been in a red office.

Me: "Hey, Narcissist, want a coffee?"

He loves coffee. The coffee approach has always been the best way to ease him into a discussion.

N: "Sure, would love some."

Me: "I'll get us some. I'll be right back. I could use your opinion on something."

A woman serving him was right up his alley. To top it off, I asked for his feedback, making him feel important.

I return to his office with two cups of coffee in hand.

Me: "Here you go. Is now a good time?"

I put down the coffee right in front of him on his desk. He's sitting behind it in his cushy custom-ordered executive chair. He smiles. He's also happy because I asked for permission to use up some of his valuable time. He winks at me.

N: "For you, always."

He motions for me to sit down. I do, first closing the door, indicating that this is a confidential conversation, then I sit so I face him at a slight angle. I lean forward with my hands around the coffee cup to indicate we are about to share some secrets and/or to show him that I'm giving him my attention.

Me: "The Widget quote."

I take a sip, watching his reaction. His eyebrow raises. He wants some good news on it. He leans forward.

N: "We got it?"

Me: "Unfortunately, no. I just saw Downer, asked if he talked with Germany."

I take another sip on purpose and look at my watch. He picks up on the hint.

N: "It's Friday. It's getting late in Germany. Did he reach them?"

Me: "He said that he couldn't get Sven to answer the phone and that he left a message."

N: "Did he call anyone else?"

Me: "Not that I know of."

He frowns, interlaces his fingers.

Me: "I asked if he had emailed them as well. It's been weeks. He didn't respond, but he did say that they won't go elsewhere because we sold them the other units. I don't believe that he sees the urgency or the problem of, once again, failing to meet a promised deadline to an important customer."

I make a point to highlight how unaffected Downer seems to be by the situation while negatively impacting Narcissist's sales potential and reputation.

He frowns again and shakes his head. His face flushes slightly.

I'm pleased that he has taken the bait so quickly.

N: "Apparently not. He should realize that the locations talk to each other, and he already had a run-in with their maintenance engineer. If we can't sell on a speedy response now, how do they feel about us when they need service, especially when the service comes from a loudmouthed, confrontative German? Customers don't like it when they are being ignored or yelled at. This is so frustrating. I have a call with Widget later. Now I'm going to have to spin a story on why we don't have a quote ready. I hate having to make excuses for him."

He frowns again, his eyebrows curl toward his nose.

I offer empathy.

Me: "Trust me. I know how you feel. It's been like this for years."

I pause and take another sip of coffee, pretending to ponder. Then, as if the thought just came to me, I say:

Me: "Too bad he doesn't work for you."

He looks at me, both eyebrows now raised. He knows I'm up to something. Still, he is intrigued. He licks his lips once while quickly glancing out of the window before looking back at me. I'm certain that he has thought of that himself, and me stating it offers him validation. He waits for me to continue.

Me: "Well, you know, it would make sense."

Internally I'm snickering, seeing that the phrase is the opposite of Downer's favorite argument.

Me: "You sell the equipment, but you need Downer to get you the quote. And he's not worried about it because what are you going to do to him? And he doesn't push his boss for the quote, because they're busy enough with quoting business in Germany."

I make a point to state how powerless he is when it comes to dealing with Downer. Plus, Narcissist always says how the Germans treat the U.S. location like dirt, so I'm affirming his opinion (trigger). He looks grim with his lips pressed together in a straight line. I continue.

Me: "And then, when you do sell equipment, you're stuck with Downer doing the installation and service calls to *your* customers. It would make sense if he reported to you. He could really use some guidance and leadership when it comes to time management and customer service. He has no boss here. There's no accountability."

Narcissist nods. He only has one other salesperson reporting to him. That doesn't satisfy his hunger for power. He hates having such a small circle of influence, and he hates having to wait on stuff when he knows he could make an easy sale. Additionally, he thinks I just complimented him on his leadership abilities.

N: "It certainly would make things easier for me."

He rubs his chin. I nod enthusiastically. The fact that it would make sense for Downer to work for Narcissist makes us allies.

Me: "It shouldn't be this hard for you to sell stuff that the customer wants so desperately. Imagine how much more business we could be gaining under your direction."

I affirm that this should be easier for HIM. I could have said for the team, but he's not interested in the team.

He nods again. Then he folds his hands and licks his lips.

N: "Well, I can run it by Napoleon when he's in a good mood. I've been thinking about it myself for a while. He is always on me for more sales, and we could be selling more if Downer would pull his weight. But . . . you know how Downer is up Napoleon's you-know-what. It would take some tweaking."

He looks straight at me, but I can tell he's focused on a thought and not my face since he doesn't blink for a while.

Me: "You're an excellent tweaker. You always know just what to say. I've tried to make my points to Napoleon about Downer's lack of performance. He doesn't believe me. Says

I'm prejudiced. I think he'll listen to you. He respects you. Remember how you could sway his opinion on the ABC situation? That itself was a small miracle."

I make the effort to stroke his ego. He smiles and then nods. He loves the compliment.

N: "Yes, I'm good with Napoleon."

Me: "Yes, you are."

I say it with enthusiasm, then I sigh.

Me: "I guess I'm just too direct. I don't know how to schmooze." I give him a sad smile. I want him to know how powerless I am.

N: "Well, you're not in sales. You can leave the schmoozing to the professionals."

Of course, he doesn't tell me what I am good at. Instead, he offers an excuse for my shortcomings while also assuring me that he's got it under control.

I waste no time to confirm his expertise. After all, he just somewhat agreed to take up my fight to eliminate, or at least control, Downer.

Me: "And so I shall."

He laughs. He winks at me.

N: "Remember . . . I take care of the front end . . ."

Me: ". . . and I take care of the back end."

It's a running joke between us. Sales is always out front, and operations is always supporting from the rear in any company.

He laughs again.

N: "Exactly."

Me: "It's a deal. You sell more and I will spend less. We could get that bonus this year. Especially if we can land Widget."

I mention *we* specifically as it sounds less greedy.

He snorts. Licks his lips, nods.

N: "It's a possibility."

I make the point to remind him that Downer is his problem and mission.

Me: "If anyone can do it, it's YOU. Despite Downer and his inabilities. Where there's a will, there's a way, right?"

He nods again.

N: "One hundred percent."

On any given day, narcissists are difficult opponents to deal with if you don't approach with caution. When confronted outside of their comfort zone, they can become defensive-aggressive quickly. It is always best to interact with them when they feel at their best and are at ease. And while narcissists can be really problematic, I find that they are easy to read and to manipulate if you can get them to align to your objectives by outlining a benefit to them or by addressing their values. Cater to them as much as possible in a way that makes them believe that they are admired and respected. You don't have to be overtly nice.

A narcissist also appreciates honesty. I had my battles with my narcissist, but he always knew where he stood if he asked. I was never afraid to speak my truth in a way that didn't endanger me, and he did the same. There are ways to be honest without giving away too much. And there are ways to acknowledge their strengths without being fake. I made sure to show my appreciation for his good accomplishments.

Because we had established honesty and trust to a degree, I was also able to share criticism without fear of retribution. It helped that we were peers as part of the management team. I could not have done this if I were his employee. As an employee to a narcissist, you must find a balance. Find their values and objectives, determine commonalities, and use them in your interactions without inference to emotions. Narcissists feed on insecurities, and when dealing with them, you must try to remain calm and centered to keep the narcissist at bay. After all, they appreciate control, and they will respect your control over your emotions—maybe not consciously—but it will change the way they see you.

I saw Narcissist as a means to an end. I was to him. I wanted the business to succeed, and so did he. While his main motivation was to make more commission on the large equipment sales, he understood that Downer was immensely damaging to the company's reputation and sales potential. I'm positive Narcissist was aware that I had a purpose by keeping myself involved in the service and sales aspect. Yet I had approached him in a nonthreatening way, showing myself to be powerless, and he felt a strong urge to act, acknowledging that he had more power in that regard than me.

My plan was simple: Every time Downer missed a quote, did not return a customer call, rescheduled service appointments, had a flare-up with a fellow teammate, made a sexist remark . . . I followed up with emails and a personal chat with Narcissist. It wasn't hard. Downer gave ample reason for nonperformance. I was always factual, but yes, I fed the fire, and I was out to trigger everyone into action. Downer, Narcissist, and Napoleon. I knew it was my job, my duty to the team and the corporate bottom line, and I went at it with focus and determination.

So . . . did I have success?

It didn't take more than a year after recruiting Narcissist to the cause for Napoleon to terminate Downer. The entire team breathed a thousand sighs of relief. Nobody missed Downer. The cancer had finally been cut out.

The above example affirms that a change in your approach to a problem can make all the difference. For years, I had asked Napoleon for help with Downer's negativity and impact. Downer was my problem, one that I could not overcome with the usual approach. Stuck in PARK. I changed my approach. It was only possible once Narcissist had been employed, and I had observed how Napoleon could be influenced by Narcissist. That observation was my NEUTRAL. I worked hard at establishing a relationship with Narcissist that was built on limited honesty and trust. I allowed him to become my DRIVE. We realized that we could accomplish a lot more by working together on certain projects, even if we didn't have much love for one another. We complemented each other with our different strengths in the pursuit of our individual goals. Narcissist was a willing participant. And we made a powerful team.

It's important for you to be aware of all the available players. You don't need to chip away at that mountain all by yourself. When you can see what others value, even if they are unpleasant people, then you can make use of that. Work smarter, not harder.

Is there more to this story? A few years after Downer got fired, I resigned. After a total of fourteen years, I had accomplished creating a dream team and achieved double-digit operational profits. In a final push, I asked to be made general manager. Napoleon refused, stating that I did not have a grasp of economics since I didn't have a college degree. A pretty good insult, seeing that I had led the company to its first positive turnover in a decade. When he slammed that ceiling on my head, that's when I started looking for another job. I had also realized that he would eventually sell the company. Some of the steps he had undertaken and some of the reports he had asked for—not to mention his interest in traveling and spending money outside of business activities—were clear indicators to me that he wanted out. It's just another example of how you need to be aware of what is going on around you to draw conclusions about what could potentially happen.

Narcissist had also expressed his desire to become general manager. I would have never worked for Narcissist, and I know that Narcissist would have never worked for me. It was a conundrum for Napoleon since he didn't want either of us to bear that title. He didn't respect me, and he didn't trust Narcissist with the company's money.

I pushed for an answer. I wanted more after having mastered my domain, and I was fed up not being rewarded or recognized. I saw my value, and it was worthy of a GM title, and I was no longer willing to settle for less. Additionally, at that point, I had decided to move forward with writing a book, and for that, I wanted to earn more money so that I could become debt-free as well as save for a sabbatical. When we were both shot down on the GM position, I actively went on a job hunt, and as luck would have it, within one month, I had a job offer. A few months after I left, Narcissist was given the GM title. However, just six months later, the company was sold to a large conglomerate. Less than a year and a half later, the U.S. facility was shut down.

Before I move on, I want to come back to these interactions for a moment. You may be surprised to learn that I had to put a lot of thought into them as I wrote them down. As a matter of fact, I had to relive each multiple times to remember more details. I also had never given them much thought during the actual encounters. That is the process I'm struggling to describe. For me, it is more intuitive than conscious effort these days. It seems a bit absurd to tell you to make the effort to notice so that you will end up not having to notice. You are not fully aware yet, but once you are, the goal is to let it happen organically based on the newfound awareness without a conscious effort of thought. It sounds crazy.

Let me try to rephrase: All that you have gathered about yourself and others—and maybe not just gathered but also acknowledged with effort and honesty—will become part of your intuition in how to best respond in the moment to the best of your capabilities, even when you are not consciously aware.

I put in the work to train my brain into automatic awareness for those times when I'm not paying attention. Our brains make so many decisions in the moment, and we are not conscious of most of them. But in your interactions, you must become aware of all the factors to drive making decisions with purpose and consciousness. If we don't consciously face those decisions with purpose—we may be too tired to make more decisions or we don't want to put in the extra effort to fight the resistance—then our brain will make the easiest decision for us based on past behaviors, not necessarily based on our values. By putting in the work to understand yourself and your core values, it will become easier for your brain to make decisions that complement and protect those values in any circumstance.

This (un)aware consciousness in decision-making could be the reason why interacting with a lot of people on any given day wears me out. It takes energy to face people with intent and to have you and your brain cooperate to strive for those outcomes that will benefit you. I can be exhausted after attending group meetings where I need to interact with multiple personalities. Again, for me, I'm aware of the drain on my battery, and typically, after such meetings, I withdraw to a quiet place for some self-care. But I also understand that I allowed my brain to work and that it had my best interest at heart (or mind).

It is worth the effort. The more you practice becoming aware of it all (learnings, observations, values, environments, circumstances, appearances, perceptions, etc.), the easier it will be for your brain to adjust and adapt in the moment. It will change its reaction and behavior if you train it to acknowledge your values when you make the effort in your own actions and reactions to change your behavior in the moment with purpose. I realize how weird it sounds, treating your brain and your actions as two different things. They currently are though, and by practicing L.O.V.E., you train them to become collaborators.

You can do so much more with the little awareness you gain every day. Nothing is ever lost or wasted if you are willing to acknowledge that. You can still value what you thought of as lost, and then make use of that for your betterment. Also, rest assured that you notice hidden signals instinctively in times of doubt, often referred to as that uneasy feeling in the pit of your stomach. If your brain cannot decide, follow your gut.

The Bad Side of Control

Control is a bit like manipulation. It can be good or bad. Emotional control is a good thing when it comes to all interactions. Naturally, we must first be aware of our emotions, as well as those of our opponent. Without emotional control, we cannot control anything else—least of all, the outcome of our interactions.

To control our emotions, we must learn about ourselves, observe and acknowledge our triggers, and then see the value of everything with awareness and honesty. The same applies to our opponent.

That type of control can become a heavy responsibility. I say that because, once you realize how you can manipulate things and people, it can result in such a powerful feeling that you could use it to do harm.

Therein lies the challenge. Once you see how in tune you are with what's happening and why, you can start tweaking the reality of an anticipated usual response. Your opponent will not notice how you are adapting, like a chameleon, to manipulate many things with intent. This process does work. And you could easily end up abusing your new powers once you see the influence you can have in your own life and others. It may sound far-fetched, but do not shrug off the potential for doing intentional harm.

Let me try to explain. I am a good manager because I can read people well enough in the moment (and in general). That's because I am willing to listen and learn about them. Their struggles, dreams, ambitions, failures, and their lives in general. I see the value in people. I can relate. I didn't learn about them to use that knowledge against them. I use that knowledge to help them, which in turn, helps me. Each person constantly broadcasts some type of data that can be observed. The awareness of my knowledge has been huge in my capabilities as a good leader in the workforce. I aim to use the data for good.

Sometimes, though, people can be real Dicks. In my years, I have gained valuable insights on my Dicks. With less awareness at first, but once I got more practice, I understood how I could also use that knowledge in a malevolent, yet satisfying, way. When confronted by an oppressor meaning to abuse me, I have acted with purpose and viciousness to defend myself by going on the attack. My intention was good (defend myself), but the execution went too far.

I have manipulated the emotions of my opponents to make them feel miserable. I have pushed them into corners with intent to watch them squirm before they lost their cool. Especially during those heated times, I forced myself to remain calm because nothing frustrates your opponent more than you keeping your composure when they go off the rails. I felt dominant and in total control, and I loved it.

When you become drunk with power, you could desire to hold on to that feeling. You could turn into the very same thing you've been trying to battle. Our victory over others should never be defined by our desire for that feeling of power or control, nor the hate we have accumulated. Additionally, there is a large element of uncertainty when you abuse your empowerment. No matter how well prepared you are for that battle, when you go at it with aggressiveness or malicious intent, then you are also forced to outsmart your opponent every step of the way. If you fail, the consequences can be dire. It's like you're playing poker and you declared yourself all in, even though you don't know all the cards on the table. As much as you try to anticipate the remaining cards, you can never ever predict them all when you attack someone maliciously. You can be prepared and still fail. Someone could outsmart you. Or that someone may become violent out of desperation. They feel that you have driven them into a corner without a choice. Never underestimate uncertainty as it can certainly get you into trouble.

I hope you can see that this can be dangerous. While some bad people may need this treatment occasionally, it should be the exception, not the rule. Remember that your relationship with that person, no matter how good or bad it was prior, will not be conducive to cooperation afterwards. This behavior will draw a definite line in the sand that will remain there indefinitely.

There's collateral damage. A power trip will destroy your integrity and your reputation. It will be hard, if not impossible, to recover. You will end up losing control because you feel so powerful in your perceived control. And with that, you will have lost all of L.O.V.E. because you are not empowering anyone with love or awareness. Your triggers are making all the decisions while you think that you have them under control.

There is no victory in tearing down another human being with hate or by controlling them with abuse.

Hate is an emotion aching for revenge. Do not confuse impact with revenge. You must let go of hate.

Time for some honesty. Some of you wouldn't be reading this book if you didn't dream about revenging or avenging yourself. And I'm with you. You want to be able to stand up to someone who has bullied you, mistreated you, abused you, threatened you. Someone who made or makes you feel small, useless, dumb, ugly, unimportant. Someone you may not be able to cut out of your life.

Instead of revenge, we shall define ourselves as the underdog making a comeback. We shall not be hateful to our haters, but we will take back what they took from us. We will right the wrong.

It's easier to hate when you don't think of them as people with lives, dreams, ambitions, families, struggles, etc. Change your viewpoint and focus on values. I addressed values throughout this book so that you are inclusive of your opponents in your decisions. They are human beings with feelings. They have families. They have struggled. You will never know the full spectrum of their lives. You cannot assume that they are simply bad to the core, which will allow you to put them in a box to justify being evil to them. That would make you no better than them. "They deserve it." Sure. Karma. I get it. But I'm saying, do not add intentional damage. Let them do their own harm by not infusing your interactions with hate. There is a difference. Learn to let go of hate as it will turn you into them.

If you have the urge to go at your opponent aggressively, then instead, give someone the benefit of the doubt. And you may just be amazed that you can get a lot done without going into the overdrive level on how badly you want to impact them. There's really no reason to go into a meeting with malicious intent to desecrate someone. Our goal is to impact ourselves by managing our interaction with them. Not impact them to where we do not value them as human beings any longer. Please keep this in mind.

How to Play the Game

It is when your opponents fail to appreciate the values and strengths of those around them—while getting intimidated by them—that games are played to protect their weak egos. Are they games though? When it impacts your life, it is no game to you. Nonetheless, you simply cannot say that you don't do games because then you admit defeat. Someone will still play the game even when you don't want to. They will benefit, and you will feel horrible and powerless. Remember, all you have to do is play the game so that you are true to yourself. To be aware of it all. To be factual and honest. Then it's no game because you changed the rules. The rules are that you play your authentic self. When you think about how games are played by others, then I hope you can see that it's just another word for manipulation. Don't be afraid of it. Playing will become a lot easier if you can create your boundaries as discussed in earlier chapters.

The Honesty in Honesty

For all of this to work, you must be honest in everything. Honesty is tricky with most people. I often show my own vulnerability by exposing the uncomfortable that nobody wants to talk about. I take pride in pointing out the obvious elephant in the room. Why not address head on what everyone is thinking about and avoiding? Of course, I am careful about the delivery (it often involves sarcasm and dark humor), and it depends on the type of people that happen to be around me. I have seen that this approach unites people, and it does open up an opportunity for honest dialogue. Use caution, though, with this approach; I'm comfortable with it because I'm aware of the dynamics of the crowd, and I'm confident that I can resolve any conflict, should it arise.

Many of you aren't ready for the truth or honesty. It all sounds good on paper. Honesty is like a new year's resolution that some attempt but never commit to longterm.

My own struggle with this book's target audience proves it. I wrote *IMPACT* to help those women who feel powerless and insecure. But I was advised (book cover expert feedback) not to put those words on the cover. My target audience, who could really benefit from L.O.V.E., could take offense if I were to call them insecure. I was told to focus on the solution instead to give it a positive spin. I get it, but I still think that it can make it tough to truly reach my target audience because that solution-driven title now could help with a lot of other issues on a broader scale. At least when I search for books, I use keywords that define my struggle, not my solution. If I knew the words to my solution, then I wouldn't need to read a book about it. While I think my book title addresses both the problem and the solution, it still feels a bit like putting lipstick on a pig. Interestingly enough, if I depicted words and images on the front cover that were bold and strong, the feedback was that my audience would also not buy the book since it looked too masculine. (What were your first thoughts when you saw the cover?)

Think about it. There is no honesty. Why do we try to appease a gender trait? Women can be strong without being masculine. Men can be soft without being feminine. We must stop assigning behavior and character traits to one gender.

People want their rosy glasses to view themselves and the world in. That doesn't work for me, and it won't work for you if you want to change. None of us are perfect. And we don't have to pretend to be better, stronger, more perfect so that other people think highly of us.

Women—Friend, Foe, or Bitch?

Women also do not need to remain enemies. I touched on this earlier in the book. Women have a hard time empowering or supporting other women. You can argue that things are changing. And I agree that there has been a slight shift. However, I would claim that you would notice this change more in the upper levels of a large company. It is the exception, not the rule.

Women want to contribute to society, and women will sacrifice themselves for the greater good. Why do women feel that others are more deserving? Women should focus on contributing to women first, and this would take care of a lot of other issues. Call it a trickle-down effect that could actually work. Somehow, though, women do not believe in themselves enough (or their society) to impact change for women to right the wrong of the continual patriarchal oppression. We do not feel we are taken seriously, we have been discouraged by everyone and the mountain seems impossible to climb, and we are confronted daily by political and religious views that benefit men. We are afraid to keep trying because we feel (and therefore are) defeated already. And so, women keep fighting the fights that are winnable for others. When we put ourselves last on purpose, no wonder that other women will not be there to support us when we try.

Have you ever thought about the woman who made it to the table with the men? Do you think there are more seats available for other women? That one woman will most likely protect her seat because she fears it will be taken away by that other woman. That other woman who may or may not be more qualified. She may be a better fit for the patriarchy's agenda, easier to control or silence by the men at that table. That seat could also be taken away by another random man. Women have fought so much to climb any ladder, and we feel constant pressure to perform better while fighting off challengers once we have arrived. We are so discouraged in totality, even after we've made it, that we can't imagine that there could be another seat at the table. And we will be too preoccupied trying to keep our seat at the table that it will also soften the impact we have. All because we cannot trust. Of course, that one woman at that table, she's still given less respect, authority, and value than the good ole boys sitting next to her. There seem to be no allies. It's like women can't win for trying.

Here's another way to look at the absence of sisterly support. Let's go back to that woman at the table, or any woman who has just achieved success. She is excited, she's on top of her world, and this is her moment to shine. She wants to forget—for a little while at least—the battles she had to fight. She has made it (for now), and she deserves to rest on her laurels without having to feel guilty about all the other women who are still struggling.

Or . . . she could simply be too tired. Exhausted by the challenges and the bigotry. She wants to rest, disengage from the mayhem. She does not want to hear about or be reminded of that huge mountain left to climb. Even though she is proof that some battles can be won, she can't bear to face the war which, in totality, still seems unwinnable. Or, as mentioned earlier, she could be too preoccupied getting ready to defend her seat. Never discount the fact that it is easy to forget or ignore your sisters when faced with the never-ending plots to demolish your success while also trying to figure out who is your friend or foe.

In case you're wondering, bitches are those who only have negative things to say anytime another woman has any success. They are neither friends nor foes. They are bitter people full of excuses. Don't be a bitch.

As a woman observing another woman's success, you need to allow her to take a breather while enjoying her victory lap. Do not put any expectations on her, and do not judge her. Give her the room and be happy for her. It is when she feels your support and acceptance that she will trust in her fellow women. It is then that she will want to do the right thing for all women. She will not forget you.

Until all of us commit to change, trust issues will persist and dominate when women organize or work together. I'm not immune to it; I have a tough time trusting women who are in peer or superior positions. I prefer working with men over women. I can read men better than women since their behavioral patterns are more straight forward. Men have privilege that affords them a level of transparency. I don't feel the same about women. I worry about the other woman's agenda, and I worry about the other woman worrying about my agenda. It's so much more complicated for women in any environment. Consider how women have to walk through life: we have to watch where we park, know the risks of walking alone at dark, carry pepper spray or know what we can use as a weapon if attacked, hold the burden of (preventing) unwanted pregnancies, watch our drinks to ensure nobody slips anything in them, hide the tampons or pads during our periods—all while worrying about how not to inspire bad behavior in men. There's a heavy burden that affects us daily, and it wears on us. Life tends to be busier for women as caretakers of others. You can't really fight when you are preoccupied trying to overcome the many (patriarchal) hurdles, zapping your energy.

Men don't have to worry as much when they go about their daily lives as far as societally imposed restrictions are concerned.

Even with all that we experience as the female gender, we still do not really trust each other. Not that we trust men either. When everyone is the enemy, I get how impossible it seems to rally women for women.

For me, men have made better allies than women because of their transparency, less complicated agendas, and obvious ambitions. Of course, a lot of men don't worry as much about losing their jobs or positions as the women working alongside them, so they can be more inclined to help women's causes. Women need to take advantage of that. While many men have been in their bubble of ignorance—afforded by male privilege—so many of them are thankful when you point out the hurdles set for women that don't exist for men. They are willing to step out and up once they are aware and understand the unlevel playing field. We must educate men, make them acknowledge their privilege (or absence of obstacles), and ask them to become allies for women specifically. Their silence and disinterest in our cause (thinking there would be no benefit to them, only less of everything) is doing us harm. Make that point. Change needs to happen in all levels, all genders, all environments. Why wouldn't we expect men to help us when we are there to support them anytime they need us? Tit for tat. Recruiting men to women's causes is crucial. The only bad men are those who fight to keep their bubble in place once you've pointed it out.

Educating men has also been easier than educating women in my experience. It sounds strange, I know. When educating men, there seems to be only one hurdle (awareness). After that, the impact on their newfound awareness can really help women. Sure, not every man will want to become aware. Some will deflect. I have found, though, that when I redirect them back to the revealed truth and ask them to sit with the thought for a few honest minutes, most will stop deflecting and turn inward. You can see it in their faces when they get it. Most had never thought to change their viewpoint, and why would they when life has been relatively easy for them? Again, do not hold it against them. It is when he is aware but unwilling to support or empower women that he shows his true colors.

The hurdle of awareness is always the first one. Women, too, can get excited over equality and equity—most of the time, it's like an explosion of pissed-off-ness when I get a bunch of them in a room, and we talk about the patriarchy—but that passion teeters out quickly once everyone goes home. It's like a raging fire turned into a pilot light. Sometimes I feel that women just want to complain about their lives, to get things off their chests, to hear that they are not alone in their struggles, and then they feel better about themselves. So much so that they are content with the status quo, and they happily coexist until someone else throws lighter fluid on that pilot flame to be ignited, once again, for a hot minute.

Experience is another hurdle for women. Experience is what puts the *but* in every solution to a problem. Experience has shown women some hurdles aren't supposed to be jumped. We are the hamsters stuck in our own wheel of stagnation. Yet the whole world would come to a stop if we simply focused on equality full-time. Women run the world behind the scenes; we bear the children needed to sustain humanity, we care, we hold it all together for everyone all the time. Life without us would NOT be possible. Fundamentally, I don't get why this has to be such a struggle if all humans want to be humane.

My intention is not to judge women harshly but to show that there are reasons that our fight is tiring and hasn't produced resounding results in decades. While progress has been made, no doubt, we still lack allies in many areas (sisterhood for one, political, legal, and financial fields for others). Of course, the more you learn about the systemic oppression of women, the easier it is to grasp the immensity of the task and how much energy it takes trying to advance women's rights or your own.

I want to make clear that it is okay to simply do as much as you can when you can, and it is also okay to step back to recharge your batteries (self-care).

The goal is for you to acknowledge that there is a past that has shaped our lives and our behaviors, and ultimately, to accept it for what it was. See what's behind an intention, a task, an ask, or a law. Acknowledge that the impacts on men and women, at times, have different purposes, benefits, or advantages. That alone can empower you and your decisions, and that is enough.

There is progress.

Women are advocating at many fronts and in many capacities. We are working on getting into (or creating allies in) governmental, legal, and political positions to drive change. We have women organizations focused on helping all women. We have more men advocating for women's causes than ever before. There is a DEI (diversity, equity, inclusion) movement educating the corporate bubble.

These approaches are working—at snail's pace, but they are meant to advance with purpose and at a tempo to support sustainable integration (takeover).

We know that men and women CAN change for the better. There is hope and a promise in that.

You can do your part. Start with yourself.

REFLECTIONS & EXERCISES

Last one. Take that previous interaction you have used as an example throughout the chapters.

Knowing and valuing your newfound understanding and awareness, what could you have done differently?

Are you able and willing to replay your sample interaction with L.O.V.E.?

Write down what you would do differently. From A to Z. There should be a lot. Would you have gone into that interaction with the same mindset and approach? Have you learned anything new or old about yourself and your opponent that has not been in your awareness previously? Can you see the environment and circumstances as influencing factors? Could you have impacted any of it prior to your encounter? Think of your body language and theirs. See it all with purpose to improve.

Imagine all scenarios.

Can you see the potential for what it can be next time?

The End & Your Beginning

Here we are. Congratulations! I hope that by now you have already seen how L.O.V.E. can impact small changes. Empowerment and sustainable results lie in the little things and in the consistency of your dedication toward becoming aware with honesty.

Interactions can have such an impact on the direction of our lives. They may not seem the most logical choice when we think about empowerment. But it's only because you haven't been the driving force behind your interactions. You were merely a participant. The empowerment behind L.O.V.E. is the simple fact that you are aware of you, them, values, goals, intentions, and feelings. L.O.V.E. will impact your life, not just your interactions. You will start loving yourself when you can learn, observe, and value who you are. Once you understand your history, experiences, and triggers (based on the framework of learning about yourself), then you can accept who you are and move forward. L.O.V.E. will stop the past from impacting your future (while using the past to impact your future).

Let's recap the L.O.V.E. steps:

Never stop **learning**. You want to continue to engage your brain cells to stay fit mentally, which ensures you can make sound decisions. Learning encompasses all aspects of your life. It's not just about reading, taking courses, continuing education, or hobbies. It's a journey of discovery: likes, dislikes, strengths, weaknesses, talents, ambitions, past experiences, feelings, dreams, etc.

Observation is such a powerful tool, underutilized by many. I hope that you can see your world with a different approach than before. There is so much information that we can take away if we observe without judgment. Observing yourself and others—by turning off the influencers around you—will empower you to make fair decisions and to remain true to yourself.

For some of you, the chapter about **value** may have been more challenging to understand. I get it. It is not easy to define value as something other than worth. All tangible items have value (humans, animals, plants, buildings, possessions). The same goes for the intangibles in life: dreams, fears, ambitions, failures, skills, talents . . . literally anything. Life—and everyone and everything in it—has purpose. Value it.

Empowerment will come when you learn, observe, and value. Trust yourself, and you will experience it. And never forget that empowerment is inclusive. You want and need allies, so educate, share, and pay it forward. Everybody wins that way.

Learn, observe, value, and empower all affect one another. I don't think you can do one of these without the presence of the others. They are so intertwined. We learn because we observe and value and because we want to become empowered while being empowered to learn. We observe because we want to learn and value and because we want to become empowered while being empowered to observe. We value because we learn and observe and because we want to become empowered while being empowered to value.

Empowerment comes from learning, observing, and valuing, yet empowerment also allows us to learn, observe, value, and empower.

You got this!

L.O.V.E. Takeaways:

1. You must self-care.
2. You are constantly learning and observing with the awareness needed to honestly and objectively analyze any data.
3. You know what emotional triggers are, and you can recognize them in yourself and others.
4. You can see value in everything and everyone.
5. You and your opponents have individual goals.
6. Your environment and circumstance have an influence on you and your opponent.
7. Your opponent is not attacking you personally.
8. Your feelings are yours, and you alone decide how you let them impact you.
9. You are not responsible for their feelings, especially if they are impacted by their own behaviors that you are using to your advantage.
10. Your actions or words cannot be driven by your emotions when interacting with those trying to oppress.
11. You must learn and rehearse facts so that you can present and reason them with logic and calm.
12. You must manipulate; the goal is not to be malicious to others so that they sustain harm that is beyond the scope of their own doing.
13. You do not see failures. Only opportunities to pivot.
14. You must support women by being honest, present, and nonjudgmental.
15. You must educate men and women.
16. You can make and engage allies while being an ally and mentor.
17. You must pay it forward. There is no empowerment without empowerment.

ABOUT ME

I'm an average woman who isn't. Just like all women.

I was born and raised near Frankfurt am Main, Germany. At the age of 18, I moved to the States where I worked in production management for decades. In 2018, fed up with "The Dick Club," I quit my job to write my first book *Dickotomy, A Dickless Memoir* (published in 2020).

L.O.V.E. represents my journey to my success and outlines my approach to living an empowered life.

I'm passionate about women's rights, and I'm dedicated to raising awareness about women's inequalities throughout both genders.

For more information visit: www.petraweiser.com.

ACKNOWLEDGEMENTS

I'm so immensely proud for seeing this book through. It has taken me more than a year with many emotional ups and downs. Some people whom I asked for advice have told me to stop wasting my time and efforts on a book that will produce no value-add income (seeing that I have not been pursuing speaking engagements or consulting opportunities). I'm not denying that I don't have a business model. I (currently) have no plans or ambition—after this book is published—to get my audience to spend (more) money on me through other means.

My goal is to empower my readers, not my bank account. *IMPACT* was published for the simple reason of wanting to impact just one person's life for the better.

There are thousands of authors (indie authors, especially) like me who write because we are passionate about something. The best thank-you that you can gift them is a review.

Just like my first book, this one is self-published. However, this go around, I made the decision to hire an editor. And I was not disappointed. Thank you to Joanna Kneller (Blue Heron Editing) for your feedback, wordsmithing, additions, clarifications, and corrections. You made this book the best version of me grammatically, and you kept me honest and reeled me back if I went too far with my generalizations (on men). You were on point when I wasn't.

Another huge thank you goes out to Flavia Dietrich for beta reading. You have helped keep me on my path and assured my inner peace with my passion project. Most authors struggle with finding beta readers, and even when they do, most will not come through. You were the fastest beta read I've ever had, and I love you for that and your awesome feedback. I appreciate the time and effort you put into all your comments, showing me that you truly did read it all!

To help attract readers, a good cover is vital. I was lucky to have been introduced to Annette Wood of Annette Wood Graphics. She acknowledged my brand (seen as offensive and profane by some), and while not obviously present in this cover, it still has the theme of *Dickless*. That's no small feat. Being true to oneself and remaining authentic while trying to attract readers who could benefit from this book has been a challenge, no doubt. Thank you, Annette, for hearing my concerns, researching my website/brand, reassuring me of my purpose and for creating this awesome cover. IMPACT is the standout bold and brave sail in the boring and compliant sea of white.

You heard me refer to horses a lot. This is thanks to my incredible horsemanship mentor Elaine Hayes of Partnership Dressage. Thanks to you, Elaine, I have been able to open my senses to EVERYTHING. Yes, that's correct. Life with horses has shown me connections that I never knew existed and which truly extend into everything. The power of animals lies in their secret language, the hidden depths of our awareness, and in the willingness to see the honesty in them and oneself.

I want to thank you, yes YOU, for reading this book. You are my reason, and without you, I have no purpose.

Finally, to my soulmate. Thank you for being you and letting me be me. Two very different individuals who are the same together. I love you more than SNICKERS Ice Cream Bars.